YOU'RE NOT HIS THERAPIST

Your No-BS Guide to Quitting Mansitting

TALI MOSS

Copyright © 2025 Tali Moss

All rights reserved.

Dedicated to

You.

For your unspoken load.

For your brilliant, buried fire.

For the day you finally said, "Enough."

May this book remind you that your needs are not negotiable, your sanity is not selfish, and you were never meant to carry it all.

You're not cold. You're not crazy.

You're just done.

And you're not alone anymore.

CONTENTS

INTRODUCTION: Stop Playing Therapist to Grown Men 7

PART I: The Job You Never Applied For 13

CHAPTER 1: The Emotional Labor Olympics 15

Emotional Labor: The Job You Didn't Know You Had 16

How You Became the Emotional CEO of Your Relationship 19

The Emotional Inequity That No One Acknowledges 21

CHAPTER 2: The Invisible Job You Somehow Signed Up For 25

How Emotional Labor Creeps In 26

Why Competence Becomes a Curse 30

No, You're Not Controlling, You're Surviving 34

CHAPTER 3: Is He Growing or Are You Shrinking? 42

The Maturity Gap: Why You Feel Like His Mother 43

What Growth Actually Looks Like 52

PART II: You Can't Fix a Grown-Ass Man 64

CHAPTER 4: Loving Potential Is How You Lose Yourself 66

The Fantasy That Keeps You Hooked 67

The Nurturer Trap 75

You're Not His Safe Space If He's Your War Zone 85

CHAPTER 5: Give Him a Fair Chance to Grow 102

Stop Fixing, Start Watching 103

Strategic Pullback Isn't Punishment, It's Permission 110

The Accountability Experiment 113

CHAPTER 6: Data Collection: Test, Don't Coddle 124

The Data Collection Phase 125

Mirror His Energy Without the Drama 130

Read the Results Like a Grown-Ass Woman 132

PART III: The Breakup With the Role, Not Just the Relationship...............145

CHAPTER 7: Put Down the Backpack, Sis 147

The Strong Woman Lie 148

Who Are You Without the Fixing? 157

What Safe Feels Like 166

Letting Go Is a Love Language 170

CHAPTER 8: The Breakup That Happens in Your Head 183

Just Because He Couldn't Love You Fully Doesn't Mean You Were Hard to Love 184

Boundaries As Self-Respect 188

You Can Release Without Bitterness 193

CHAPTER 9: When Walking Alone Starts to Feel Lighter......................197

Returning to Yourself 198

It's Not Weak to Miss Him. It's Human 201

Walking Away Doesn't Mean You Wanted To 212

PART IV: Your Comeback Era Starts Now 219

CHAPTER 10: The Why: Neuroscience of Emotional Hunger...................223

The Rubber Band Theory 224

He Wasn't Taught to Show Up, He Was Taught to Shut Down 229

How Society Screwed You Both 235

CHAPTER 11: Redefining Love 241

Rewrite the Fairy Tale 242

Green Flags & Grown Standards 252

Staying Open Without Losing Yourself 261

CONCLUSION: This Isn't About Him, It's About You Finally Coming Home to Yourself 273

References 281

INTRODUCTION:

STOP PLAYING THERAPIST TO GROWN MEN

I want to be clear from the get-go: this is not a book about hating men. It is a book about loving yourself enough to stop carrying what is not yours. If the title made you brace for a rant, relax. I am not here to bash men. I am here to hand you back your peace.

Why mansitting is a national epidemic: smart women everywhere are burning out from babysitting grown men. I'm seeing it every bloody day! And just like them, you did not sign up to be his mother, coach, or therapist. Yet here you are, doing unpaid emotional labor like it is a second job you never applied for. You soothe, you explain, you remind, you manage. Every time you try to step back, he looks at you like you are cruel for leaving him to fend for himself.

That invisible burden has a name: **emotional labor**. Picture it like a backpack stuffed with everyone else's needs. Inside are the birthdays you remember, the appointments you schedule, the pep talks you give, and the eggshells you walk on when his moods hit. You started by carrying one or two small things. Now the bag is so heavy you can barely stand up straight.

This book is not a fairy tale and it's going to sting in places you didn't know you had. It is a manual for peace and self-respect. No more spreadsheets of his potential. No more unpaid therapy sessions disguised as date night. No more years wasted waiting for him to wake up.

What you will find here:

- **Language** to finally name what has been draining you, so you stop questioning your sanity and start trusting your gut.

- **Tools** to draw bold, unapologetic boundaries, and the backbone to hold them when tested.

- **A clear picture** of what partnership should look like, so you can stop gaslighting yourself into thinking scraps are a feast.

- **The courage** to give him one real chance to step up, and the clarity to walk if he does not.

- **Practical strategies** to shift the emotional load without burning your life down in the process.

- And above all, a **solid path back to yourself**, whether you stay, go, or rewrite the rules entirely.

Again, this book is not here to vilify men. Masculinity comes with its own pressures, and plenty of men want to show up better. Some just do not know how. Others do, but refuse. **The distinction matters.**

What matters more is this: you are allowed to put yourself first. You are allowed to want a relationship that does not feel like babysitting. You are allowed to stop twisting yourself into a pretzel to keep someone else comfortable. If you start wondering **how**, keep reading.

Why did I write this book? Because I have heard the same story on repeat. Women I know and women I barely know, whispering (some screaming) the same tune:

"I feel like the adult in my relationship, and I am tired."

"I love him, I just wish someone looked after **me** for once."

"Maybe I am asking for too much."

"This is what means to be a good woman."

These women are not weak. They are loyal, capable, and emotionally generous. And they are **exhausted**. I saw myself in their stories, and maybe you see yourself too.

If something this common feels this heavy, it is not a personal problem. **It is a pattern.** One we do not talk about nearly enough.

So if you are ready to stop overfunctioning, you are in the right place. You might feel scared, you might be clinging to hope, you might be worried you are too much. You are not. You are just finally noticing how heavy the load has been. And you are ready to put it down.

This book begins with truth, with clarity, and with power. A middle finger to the role you never asked for, and an open heart to the peace you are about to claim.

You are not his therapist. You are tired. And that is about to change.

PART I:

THE JOB YOU NEVER APPLIED FOR

CHAPTER 1:

THE EMOTIONAL LABOR OLYMPICS

Emotional Labor: The Job You Didn't Know You Had

Let me tell you about Kaitlin.

She's one of the most capable women I know. Smart, organized, resilient to her core. She's been in a relationship for almost a decade with a man who is deeply creative and sensitive, but also emotionally unstable. His childhood was full of trauma. The kind that doesn't just disappear, it leaves a mark. And he's carried that mark into adulthood like an open wound.

He leans on her. For everything. She manages their life, their bills, their appointments, their emotional climate. When she needs help… when she's overwhelmed, grieving, exhausted, he can't show up. Not because he doesn't care, but because he genuinely doesn't know how. Stress makes him implode. Any kind of conflict or tension sends him into a spiral. He blames her. He explodes. He apologizes. And then it happens all over again.

The most brutal example? She recently had a health emergency and he had to take her to the hospital. But instead of being her rock, he became another weight to carry. He panicked. He lashed out. He made the entire experience so stressful, so chaotic, that she later told me she wished he hadn't come at all. Imagine that: the moment you're most vulnerable, and the person who's supposed to have your back just adds to your crisis.

She loves him. She really does. She wants him to heal. She wants him to be happy. But in the process of holding both of their emotional loads, she's slipping. And he doesn't even see it.

You don't have to have her exact story to recognize the feeling, that subtle shift from partner to parent.

That's emotional labor. It's what you're doing when you:

- Anticipate his moods and adjust yours to accommodate them

- Smooth over awkward moments in public so no one sees the cracks

- Keep track of every social plan, life admin, and practical task

- Offer emotional support even when you're the one who's breaking

It's exhausting. And the worst part? You probably didn't even realize you were doing it.

It starts slow… he forgets something, and you cover. He melts down, and you soothe. He's struggling, and you step up. And before you know it, you're doing the work of two adults while he coasts through, cushioned by your competence.

And the world still pretends women wouldn't know what to do without a man to lead them through chaos. Phhhlease.

Remember how Reese Witherspoon once called out that tired script moment where, mid-crisis, the woman turns to the man and gasps, *"What do we do now?"*

And her response? ***"Do you know any woman in any crisis situation who has absolutely no idea what to do?*** *I mean, come on. It's RIDICU-LOUS that a woman wouldn't know what to do!"*

Exactly.

That helpless, arm-clutching trope doesn't exist in real life, not among the women I know. When the shit hits the fan, we're not looking around for someone to take the lead. We **are** the lead. We're triaging in real time. Handling paperwork while processing trauma. Driving through tears with one hand and Googling symptoms with the other. Remembering everyone's damn Medicare number while managing the emotional volatility of the man in the passenger seat.

And then we're called "too emotional." Imagine that. Jeez, it makes my ears steam like a choo-choo train!!

This section is here to say: **you're not imagining it.** You're not overreacting. You're not cold or controlling. You're just tired. You've been carrying a job title no one acknowledged, managing an emotional infrastructure no one even sees.

In the next section, we'll dig into how exactly you ended up here, and why it's not your fault. But first, let this sink in: If you've ever felt like you're running the entire emotional household, it's because you probably are.

And you don't owe anyone an apology for starting to let go.

How You Became the Emotional CEO of Your Relationship

No one handed you a clipboard and said, "Congratulations! You're now responsible for managing this man's emotional well-being, calendar, self-esteem, and ability to function as a human." And yet, here you are.

You didn't walk into your relationship looking for a second job. But bit by bit, responsibility crept into your hands. Why? Because you're good at it. Because you love him. Because someone had to keep things from falling apart, and you were the only one who knew how.

But the truth is: **women are socialized to step up**. From a young age, you were likely taught to be the caretaker, the peacekeeper, the emotionally intuitive one. While little boys were praised for being brave or funny, little girls were told to be helpful, kind, and considerate. That conditioning doesn't just vanish when we start dating… it deepens. It sets us up to see our partner's growth as our **personal project**.

And if you're a high-functioning, emotionally intelligent woman? Oh, you're screwed, babe. You spot the red flags, but you empathize with them. You see the pain behind the dysfunction. You want to help. So, you do.

Here's what that "help" starts to look like:

- You start managing not just your own emotions, but his too.

- You cushion your words to avoid setting him off.

- You take on more because he's "going through something."

- You coach him through his insecurities while minimizing your own needs.

- You become the emotional anchor, the logistical planner, the soft place to land, and eventually, the last line of defense between him and collapse.

And let's not forget how love can blur the line. You love him, so you want to support him. You want him to feel safe with you. That's beautiful. But when that love turns into a full-time emotional service job with no reciprocation? That's when it stops being intimacy and starts being labor.

The hardest part? **He might not even realize it's happening**. To him, it just feels like things "work." He doesn't see that they only work because you're spinning plates behind the scenes, managing both of your emotional ecosystems like a backstage crew trying to keep the show from falling apart.

This isn't a blame game, it's a visibility issue. You're doing so much, and no one's calling it what it is: unpaid, unrecognized emotional management.

You didn't apply for this promotion to CEO of the Relationship. But once you accepted it, even unconsciously, it became hard to put down. Now it's time to look at how you can.

The Emotional Inequity That No One Acknowledges

I used to pride myself on being low-maintenance. Until I realized low-maintenance just meant I had no room to need anything.

And here's where it gets really frustrating: not only are you managing the emotional climate of your relationship, but you're doing it so well that no one even notices. Not him. Not your friends. Not your in-laws. Maybe not even you, not fully. Until you're so burnt out, the idea of one more emotional emergency makes you want to fake your own death and move to Portugal.

The emotional inequity is so normalized that when you bring it up, people tilt their heads and say, "But isn't that just what relationships are?" No. That's what unbalanced, emotionally one-sided relationships are. And they're draining the life out of women everywhere.

Let's break this down:

- **He gets space to feel, you get labeled "too much."** He can have an off day and withdraw into silence for hours, maybe days, and it's chalked up to "processing." You raise your voice once, and suddenly you're being "dramatic" or "nagging."

- **He gets empathy, you get expectations.** If he's overwhelmed, people rally around him. If you're overwhelmed, you're expected to power through. It's assumed you'll be fine. That you always are.

- **He gets to be fragile, you have to be functional.** You're allowed to be vulnerable, *but only after* you've made sure everyone else is okay first. If you break, everything breaks, so you don't.

- **He gets praise for basic effort.** If he takes the initiative even once, people act like he discovered fire. Meanwhile, your daily grind of planning, managing, and soothing goes completely unacknowledged, because you make it look effortless.

This inequity isn't just unfair. It's isolating. It breeds quiet resentment. It kills intimacy. It turns you into a caretaker instead of a partner. And slowly but surely, it chips away at your sense of self. You start asking less, needing less, shrinking to fit the emotional gaps he won't step into.

And the worst part? When you finally speak up, when you finally say, "Hey, I'm drowning here," you might still get met with confusion, defensiveness, or a well-meaning apology that changes nothing. Because emotional inequity isn't always malicious. It's just deeply ingrained. And it won't fix itself.

So no, you're not imagining it. You're not asking for too much. You're just asking not to be the only adult in the room.

And that is more than reasonable.

You've seen the load. You've named it. Next, we'll talk about how it crept in, because burnout doesn't happen overnight; it happens drip by drip.

CHAPTER 2:

THE INVISIBLE JOB YOU SOMEHOW SIGNED UP FOR

How Emotional Labor Creeps In

How Small Favors Turn Into Lifelong Roles

It usually starts with something small. He forgot to call the plumber, so you did it. He got overwhelmed by a work deadline, so you handled dinner and the laundry. He forgot his mom's birthday, so you reminded him, and sent the gift while you were at it. You didn't mind at the time. You love him. It felt natural to step in.

A favor became a habit. The habit became a pattern. The pattern became a quiet **transfer of responsibility**.

Because you were capable, because you cared, because you made it look easy, he assumed you'd keep doing it. And you did, because someone had to.

Suddenly you're not just helping, you're **project managing**. You're reminding, planning, anticipating. You're not just doing your share, you're doing his too, plus the mental load of keeping it all afloat.

Here's what that often looks like:

- You don't wait for him to forget things, you preemptively handle them.

- You don't complain, because it's faster to do it yourself.

- You tell yourself he's not good at this stuff and quietly let him off the hook.

He may not be plotting it. He's fallen into a rhythm that benefits him and quietly suffocates you. Because you make it work, he assumes everything's fine.

But it's not fine. You're drowning. You're exhausted. And when you finally say you need help, you're met with confusion or guilt, or worse, a defensive "But I thought you liked doing that?"

That first little favor? It was just the entry point to a job you never interviewed for, but somehow became entirely responsible for.

"Helping Out" vs. Silently Absorbing Responsibility

Here's where the shift gets sneaky. At first, you were just helping out. He was tired. Stressed. Busy. You picked up a few things to keep things moving. But somewhere along the line, that "help" hardened into expectation.

You became the default. Not because you announced it. But because you never dropped the ball.

Helping out looks like teamwork. It's conscious, collaborative, and acknowledged. Absorbing responsibility, on the other hand, is when the mental load shifts so gradually that it becomes invisible… even to you. Suddenly you're the one:

- Always planning ahead

- Noticing what needs to be done

- Following up, following through, and carrying the stress of the "what ifs"

You don't remember when it happened. It's not like he said, *"You handle everything from now on."* But that's exactly what's happened. You don't get to just "help out" anymore. You run the ship. He's just on board.

Because you do it so well, so silently, it never looks like a burden. Until you're burning out. Until you're crying in the car because you forgot one thing and no one else even noticed the fifty things you kept together.

Let's call this what it is: a quiet shift from collaboration to emotional outsourcing. And the longer it goes unchecked, the harder it becomes to even ask for help, because somewhere deep down, you've started to believe this is just your job.

It's not. And it never was.

The Moment You Realized You're Doing Everything

Sometimes it hits you quietly. Other times it slaps you across the face like a cold bucket of water. One day, you're rushing around trying to juggle ten things at once: groceries, work, your mom's birthday, his bad mood, and you ask him to handle **just one** thing. Something simple. Call the vet. Book the car in. Pick up the gift.

And he says: *"Can you just do it?"*

That's the moment. The snap. The *BOOM*. Your brain flashes through everything you've been doing, managing, remembering, organizing, fixing, adjusting, absorbing.

You're not a partner, you're a one-woman production team. You're not **in** a relationship, you're **running** it. And worse, it's so normalized that he thinks asking you to "just do it" is a reasonable request. He has no idea he's standing on a foundation you built, maintained, and patched together with your own time, energy, and mental bandwidth.

You've seen the script. *Everybody Loves Raymond. King of Queens.* The charmingly helpless husband, the exhausted wife who quietly runs the whole operation while the laugh track claps. Cute on TV. In real life, it's unpaid overtime. And suddenly you realize: it's all on you. All of it.

Not just one missed chore or a forgotten errand. It's the weight of everything behind it. It's the years of *"can you just," "I forgot," "you're better at this than me,"* and *"I didn't know it mattered."* It's the accumulation of invisible labor that suddenly becomes **very** visible, all at once.

That moment isn't just anger. It's grief, the heartbreak of realizing you've been disappearing inside a role that doesn't love you back.

And once you see it, you can't unsee it.

Good. Don't. That clarity? It's your way out. And that's probably the reason why you're reading this book.

Why Competence Becomes a Curse

Now that we've named the load, let's look at what leads to it. Let's talk about one of the cruelest ironies in emotional labor: the better you are at managing life, the more invisible your labor becomes, and the more is silently expected of you.

I thought I was **really good at life.** I was just making it easy for someone else not to try.

How Being Good at Managing Life Becomes a Trap

You're the responsible one. The planner. The one who remembers birthdays, anticipates moods, stocks the fridge, sends thank-you texts, follows up on everything, and still somehow manages to look like you've got it all together. At least from the outside.

But here's the trap: because you **can** do it all, people assume you *should.* And then they start handing you more.

Your partner forgets something — no problem, you've already handled it. He drops the ball — doesn't matter, you caught it. Over time, your competence becomes your curse. You start to feel like the relationship's success is tied directly to your capacity to stay ahead of the mess.

And because you *do* stay ahead of it, because you're good at it, he never even notices the mess was there to begin with.

What starts as helpful turns into **essential.** What starts as support turns into survival. You become the default, the fixer, the fallback plan. And while he gets to live in the comfort of everything "just working out," you're quietly running triage behind the scenes.

The world praises you for being the strong one. But no one stops to ask what it's costing you to keep showing up that way. Least of all him.

This is where we start shifting things. Not because you're not capable, but because you shouldn't have to carry it all just because you **can**.

Why "Strong Women" Get the Short End of the Emotional Stick

Here's the cruel paradox: the stronger you are, the less support you get. You're so good at keeping it together that no one even thinks to ask what would happen if you stopped.

You've become the emotional vault. The one everyone leans on. The one who always has the answers. You've built a reputation around being resilient, reliable, composed, whether you feel that way or not. And that image? It's become your emotional straightjacket.

Because if you're the "strong one," then who do you get to lean on? Who catches you when you fall, if falling isn't even considered an option?

Being strong isn't the problem. The problem is that your strength has been mistaken for infinite capacity. And when people think you're built to handle everything, they stop offering you the soft place to land.

It also doesn't help that society romanticizes strong women as if we're mythical creatures who thrive on struggle. As if the emotional labor is a badge of honor, not a burden. You don't get celebrated for setting boundaries. You get celebrated for powering through, even when you're crumbling.

But here's the truth: being strong shouldn't mean suffering in silence. It shouldn't mean you carry everyone else's emotional weight while no one bothers to ask how **you're** doing.

Your strength is not an invitation for others to check out. And it's not your job to keep proving it.

Perfection Is a Trap: The More Seamless You Make It, the Less He Sees It

There's a brutal irony in emotional labor: the better you are at it, the less visible it becomes. And the more invisible it is, the less it's appreciated. That's the trap. That's how you end up doing **everything** without anyone even noticing.

You don't get thanked for preventing chaos. You don't get recognized for running mental logistics like a silent backstage crew. You don't get seen, because you're too damn good at making it all look easy.

And let's be real: you didn't set out to be perfect. You set out to make life manageable. You stepped in to smooth things over because someone had to. Because things fall apart without you. But what started as competence turned into a curse. You became the emotional duct tape holding the whole damn relationship together—and he just got used to the fix always being in.

It's not that he's ungrateful on purpose. It's that your perfectionism built a system where he **never had to see the cracks.** And when things **seem** to be working, why would he question it?

So, he doesn't see how many mental tabs you've got open. He doesn't see the emotional bracing you do before every conversation. He doesn't see the planning, the buffering, the internal negotiations you run every bloody day. He just sees a calm surface and assumes there's no storm.

Perfection is a brilliant disguise. It hides how exhausted you are. It masks how much effort it takes to keep things functional. And it gives him permission… not maliciously, but by default — to stop trying. Because you've got it. You **always** have it.

Until you don't.

Until something breaks. Until you cry on the bathroom floor because one forgotten birthday or one thoughtless comment becomes the straw that cracks your composure. And when you finally break down, he's confused. *"But you never said anything was wrong."*

Of course you didn't. **Perfection doesn't complain. Perfection doesn't crack. Perfection doesn't get to be human.**

And that's what this chapter is calling out: the cost of seamlessness. The emotional labor of invisibility. You were sold the **cool girl** myth as the way to earn love. But in reality, it's the way to disappear.

You don't need to be a perfect partner. You need to be a visible one. Messy, real, vocal. Imperfect, but whole. That's how you stop carrying the emotional weight in silence, and start demanding a relationship where both people show up, mess and all.

No, You're Not Controlling, You're Surviving

You Asked Once. Then Twice. Now You're "Nagging."

It starts the same way. You ask nicely. A simple reminder. A calm request. *"Hey, could you please take care of that?"* You're not trying to micro-manage, just trying to share the load.

He says, "Sure." And then… nothing happens. You wait. You hope. You give him space to follow through. Still nothing.

So, you ask again. This time, with a little edge in your voice. Because the trash is still sitting there. The bill is still unpaid. The conversation you needed to have is still floating in the air like smoke.

Suddenly you're **nagging**.

You weren't yelling. You weren't scolding. You were reminding. Following up. Trying to make life work without everything falling on your shoulders. But the minute you ask more than once, **you** become the problem. Not the unhandled task. Not the emotional avoidance. You.

It's freakin' infuriating.

Because we all know, if you didn't follow up, it wouldn't get done. And then what? You'd be blamed for "letting it slip" or living in the consequence of his inaction. Either way, you lose. So, what do you do? You keep tracking it. You keep holding the clipboard. You become the human calendar, the appointment setter, the feelings manager.

And then… when you **finally** snap? When you've asked the same thing three, four, five times and your voice raises an octave? Now you're "too intense." Now you're "overreacting." Now he says, *"God, I was gonna do it, you didn't have to get all worked up."*

But that's the thing: if he was going to do it, he would've done it already.

Follow-through is character, not calendar.

What he doesn't understand is that every follow-up, every reminder, every repeated request, it's not about the **thing**. It's about what the thing represents: that your time doesn't matter. That your needs come last. That he expects to be asked **several times** before acting, while you're expected to intuitively handle everything on your own.

Let's make one thing clear: **being forced to manage what he won't isn't controlling. It's surviving.**

It's protecting your peace. It's trying to stay afloat in a relationship where tasks and emotions don't get shared, they get dropped. And you're the one who keeps catching them.

You're not a nag. You're a woman tired of repeating herself in a house that doesn't seem to hear her until she's yelling.

And maybe, just maybe… it's time to stop yelling. Not because you're wrong. But because you've realized you're the only one still trying to make this work like a team.

Boundaries Aren't Micromanagement, They're Clarity

Let's get something straight: asking for what you need is not controlling. Setting a boundary is not an attack. Following through on a limit doesn't make you "rigid" or "too much."

It makes you clear.

But somehow, when a woman says *"no,"* or *"this doesn't work for me,"* or *"I'm not doing that anymore,"* she gets labeled controlling, cold, demanding. "Difficult." That favorite insult tossed around whenever a woman stops softening herself to make someone else comfortable.

You've probably been there. You asked him not to raise his voice when you're disagreeing. You said you don't want to be the one managing his appointments anymore. You made it clear that if he's going to keep canceling plans at the last minute, you're going to stop making them. And suddenly — boom. You're "too intense," "hard to please," or "always on edge."

But here's the truth no one says out loud: **they only call it controlling when the control you're taking is over your own damn life.**

A boundary isn't a rule you force on someone. It's a **line you draw for yourself.** It's saying, "I'm not going to stay in a situation where I'm treated like an afterthought," not, "You have to change everything you do." He **can** raise his voice, but then you'll leave the room. He **can** ignore responsibilities, but you won't keep cleaning up the mess.

Boundaries are not manipulation. They're not ultimatums. They're **data points** for what you're no longer willing to tolerate.

The problem? **A lot of men have never been taught to hear a boundary without personalizing it.** They think your limit is a punishment. They treat your standard like a rejection. They hear "you can't do that" instead of "I'm not going to absorb the cost of this anymore."

So, you soften your edges. You rewrite your needs to make them palatable. Your clear **no** becomes a polite maybe, just to keep the peace. But peace built on silence is not peace. It's tension in disguise.

Real love wants clarity. Real partnership doesn't resent boundaries, it respects them. The man who truly sees you won't get defensive when you draw a line. He'll get curious. He'll meet you there. He won't see your standards as demands, he'll see them as a **guide to knowing and loving you better.**

You're not here to tiptoe around his sensitivities while ignoring your own exhaustion. You're not here to carry the weight of the relationship and then be called controlling for asking him to carry **literally anything**.

A boundary isn't a power move. It's a survival skill. And frankly, it's overdue.

Inconsistency Breeds Hypervigilance. You Didn't Choose This Job.

Let's talk about the kind of emotional labor that doesn't show up on a to-do list but still consumes you: the constant scanning, second-guessing, adjusting. The quiet, invisible work of trying to predict what version of him you're going to get today.

Will he be engaged and loving? Detached and irritable? Silent and sulking? Or weirdly fine for no reason and you have to act like the last three days didn't just happen?

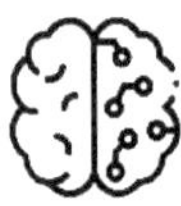

Neuroscience in Action

Chronic inconsistency trains the nervous system to expect threat. The brain can't tell the difference between relational uncertainty and real danger, so your stress response fires early and often.

You're not overreacting. You're over-conditioned.

You read him like weather. A tone shift and your shoulders tense. A sigh that's too loud? You brace for impact. A delay in response? You start replaying the last thing you said.

This isn't love. This is hypervigilance. And it doesn't happen by accident.

It happens when **his inconsistency trains you** to be constantly on alert. To scan the emotional horizon. To anticipate storms before they hit. To adjust **your** behavior to avoid setting him off, even when nothing you did was wrong.

And then, just to twist the knife, he calls you dramatic. Controlling. Overthinking. He tells you to "relax," that "everything's fine," even as your nervous system is screaming otherwise.

Let's be clear: you didn't choose this job. You didn't wake up one day and decided to become the emotional quality control manager of your relationship. You were **forced into that role** because he's unpredictable, and when people are unpredictable, the only way to survive is to stay three steps ahead of every potential fallout.

And let's be honest, it's exhausting.

And the worst part? You probably think this hyperawareness is your fault. That you're the anxious one. That you're too sensitive. That maybe if you just communicated better, or stayed calmer, or gave him more space, things would be easier.

But what if I told you your hypervigilance isn't a flaw?

It's a symptom. Of an environment that doesn't feel safe. Of a dynamic where your needs are inconsistently met. Of a relationship where the emotional ground is always shifting beneath your feet.

In healthy relationships, you don't have to guess how your partner will show up. You don't have to over-explain, over-function, or pre-emptively solve problems that aren't yours. You don't live in survival mode.

But when consistency is missing, you adapt. Not because you're controlling, but because you're trying not to get hurt.

So no, **you're not a micromanaging mess**. You're a woman who's learned how to walk on emotional landmines while smiling.

Step off the battlefield. Chapter 3 is where we name the identity you built to survive it.

CHAPTER 3:

IS HE GROWING OR ARE YOU SHRINKING?

The Maturity Gap: Why You Feel Like His Mother

Why Emotional Development Isn't Gender-Neutral

Men and women were not raised with the same emotional starter pack. Not even in the same zip code. While you were being taught to scan the room for everyone else's comfort level before deciding if it was okay to speak, he was being taught to push every single emotion down into his chest cavity and slam the lid shut like it was top secret intel.

So when you ask him to talk about his feelings and he stares at you like you've just spoken ancient Greek, he's not trying to be a dick. He's genuinely lost. Because no one ever taught him how to care **out loud**.

This emotional mismatch didn't start with you. It started when you were five, and someone told you to "be nice" when a boy pulled your hair. It started when he was told to "man up" after he cried because his dog died. Girls were handed the invisible instruction manual on how to keep everyone emotionally regulated while boys were handed... what? A soccer ball and a handshake?

We were socialized into **opposite realities**. You got handed the empathy toolkit with ten different words for sadness and guilt-trips for using any of them. He got handed duct tape and the phrase "Get over it."

So, fast-forward a couple of decades. You're in a relationship, and you're fluent in nuance, body language, unsaid needs, and vibe shifts. You've been reading emotional subtext since you were old enough to mediate family dinners. Meanwhile, he's still stuck at *"I'm fine"* with the emotional range of a potato on mute.

And then... You get told you're too emotional, too sensitive, too much. While he gets standing ovations for admitting, once, three years ago… that work has been "kinda stressful lately."

What the actual fuck?

Let's stop pretending this is about intelligence. **It's about fluency. Emotional fluency.** And while you were forced to become a multi-lingual master of feelings and facial expressions just to keep your family from combusting, he's been praised for offering up one vague sentence and not storming out.

So, when you say *I need support*, what you mean is: **be present, stay here, stop shutting down, stop making this about feeling attacked. Get it.**

And what he hears is: I'm failing. I'm bad. I'm in trouble. Abort mission.

Because no one ever told him that being emotionally present isn't weak, it's intimate. No one showed him that sitting in hard feelings without trying to fix or flee is the strongest thing you can do. No one taught him that "I'm struggling" is not an admission of failure but an invitation to connect.

So yes, you feel the gap. And no, you're not being a snob. You've just been living on a different emotional planet.

Backed by Science

Across cultures, boys are more often discouraged from naming feelings and more often reinforced for emotional suppression. Over time, suppression reduces **emotional vocabulary** and increases **shutdown or reactivity** under stress.

Translation: many men aren't incapable. **They're undertrained.** Fluency is learnable, not magic.

You were the one holding space, reading the room, checking the tone, drafting the apology text, de-escalating your mom, decoding your best friend's silence, and somehow still wondering if **you're** the dramatic one.

He, on the other hand, was raised to *ignore* discomfort unless it involved a broken bone or a car engine. He was taught to shut it down, numb it out, brush it off, or lash it back onto whoever dared bring it up.

So, when he blanks, crumbles, or explodes in the face of vulnerability, it might not be because he doesn't care. It might just be that he doesn't know how to be there without falling apart. That's emotional illiteracy. And while it's not always his fault, it **is** his responsibility.

Let me say this out loud: **you are not his teacher.**

You can offer space, model depth, show presence... without performing open-heart surgery every time you speak a need.

But you do not have to shrink. You do not have to mother him into maturity. You do not have to trade your peace for his potential.

The gap may not be his fault. But closing it? That's his damn job.

Signs You're Parenting Your Partner

It doesn't hit you all at once. It creeps in slowly, almost invisibly, until one day you're lying in bed, staring at the ceiling, wondering why you feel more like a middle manager with maternal instincts than a woman in a grown-up relationship.

Because no, it doesn't come with a diaper bag or lullabies. But it shows up in your Google calendar, where you've logged **his** dentist appointment. It shows up in the quiet way you rehearse a text ten different ways to avoid triggering one of his infamous sulks. It shows up in the tension headache you get from constantly anticipating what he's going to forget, drop, ignore, or deflect next, and deciding to handle it yourself before it turns into yet another exhausting conversation.

And it shows up in the sinking realization that if you vanished for a week, the entire operation that is your shared life would collapse faster than you can say 'Oh shit!'

If you feel more like a caretaker than a companion, chances are — you are.

Let's take the gloves off and call it what it is. You:

- Remind him to pay the rent on time like he's your teenage son.

- Schedule his check-ups like his goddamn PA.

- Run emotional interference every time he's had "a rough day," so you cushion your needs until he's in a better mood (yeah, he never is).

- Know his food intolerances better than your own.

- Adjust your tone like you're a hostage negotiator, trying to avoid another shutdown, freak-out, or pity spiral.

- Rewrite your own sentences mid-conversation because he "takes things the wrong way."

You're not in a relationship. You're running an unpaid emotional pre-school.

And he's not evil. He's not even trying to be manipulative (most of the time). He's just figured out, consciously or not, that he doesn't *have* to stay on top of anything, because you've already got it covered. All of it. Every reminder, every repair, every emotional thread in the tapestry of daily life.

And you? You're damn tired. But letting go feels scarier than holding on, because deep down, you don't actually trust him not to mess everything up if you stop holding it together. That's not love. That's project management in heels.

But there's a difference: **in parenting, the goal is to raise someone into independence. In your relationship? You're just spinning your wheels while he gets to coast.**

Because the longer you carry the emotional weight for two people, the less space there is for you to rest, recharge, or even remember what it feels like to be **received** instead of managed.

And if you've noticed your sex drive evaporating like a sad puddle in the sun, let me hand you a brutally honest truth: **you can't feel turned on by someone you're subconsciously mothering.** You're not going to get hot and bothered for a man you also have to remind to take his multivitamin.

So, let's lay it out: if you're constantly walking on eggshells, softening your language, overcompensating for his lack of follow-through, and handling everything from his appointments to his apologies, you're not just "helping out." You are mothering a grown-ass man who should know better.

And the more you over-function, the more you rob both of you of a real, adult relationship built on reciprocity instead of resentment.

Because **you didn't sign up to be a mom with benefits. You signed up to be a woman who gets to be held, heard, and seen, not just useful.**

So if this stings a little, that's okay. It means you're waking up. It means the mask is slipping and you're starting to see the dynamic for what it is. And once you see it, you have the power to stop playing into it.

You can stop explaining things he should already know. You can stop softening your needs to avoid his discomfort. **You can stop managing his damn life like your love depends on it.**

You don't have to stay trapped in the parent role just because it feels familiar. You can step out of it. Slowly, consciously, and unapologetically.

And when you do, you'll finally give him the one thing he actually needs if he ever wants to grow up: **the space to feel the consequences of being underdeveloped.**

When Love Feels Like Babysitting

There's a moment, and maybe it was this morning, or maybe it's been slowly building for years, when you find yourself looking at the man you once wanted to rip the clothes off of and thinking: *I swear to God, if I have to explain how the laundry basket works one more time, I'm going to set it on fire.*

That's not love talking. That's **babysitter fatigue**.

You used to fantasize about weekends away, spontaneous sex, or at least a thoughtful conversation over dinner. Now? You fantasize about him remembering to buy toilet paper without a goddamn reminder. Or rinsing the dishes before they start growing a new civilization. Or, just once, managing his own moods without dragging yours down with him.

Love isn't a 24/7 supervision shift. You shouldn't have to mentally brace yourself every time something mildly stressful happens in his life, because you know the meltdown's coming. You know you'll be the one calming it down. You'll be the one fixing it, translating it, absorbing it.

And girl, just admit — you've started to resent the fact that your partner is somehow more exhausting than your actual kids.

This is the part no one wants to say out loud: when you're doing the emotional labor for two, romantic love starts to feel like unpaid overtime. The tenderness gets replaced with tension. The attraction dries up. And before you know it, the man you once curled up next to like a home has become just another task to manage.

And it's not just the to-do list. It's the **tone of the relationship**. You tiptoe around his bad moods and downplay your own needs because you're already maxed out meeting his. You lower your expectations so you don't have to be disappointed… again.

That's not love. That's survival mode.

And if you're sitting there wondering why you feel tired all the time, why you've stopped wanting to touch him, or why your nervous system spikes every time he says *"Can we talk?"* — it's because your body knows what your brain is still trying to deny:

This doesn't feel like a partnership anymore. It feels like parenting.

Romance can't breathe in a nursery.

And the worst part? You probably still love him. Deeply. You see the good in him. You remember the potential. You're not here because you're cold-hearted biatch. You're here because **you care.** So, you keep doing the work. You keep holding the space. You keep picking up the pieces, and hoping maybe this time he'll finally see how heavy it is.

Love isn't supposed to feel like a second job with no days off. It's supposed to be where you go to **rest**.

So, ask yourself:

- Are you constantly coaching him through emotional basics?

- Are you the only one who notices tension, smooths it out, and circles back?

- Are you the keeper of peace, order, and emotional sanity while he gets to just… **be?**

If so, you're not building a relationship. You're building a day care center in your living room. And the longer you do it, the more you disappear. The more you become a manager instead of a woman. A caretaker instead of a partner.

But you don't have to keep doing it.

You don't have to shrink your needs down to a level that fits his capacity. You don't have to keep trading intimacy for "keeping the peace." You don't have to parent a grown-ass man just because he never learned how to show up.

You are not crazy. You are not demanding. You are **done mansitting**.

Love should be where you exhale, not where you go to hold your breath.

What Growth Actually Looks Like (And What It Doesn't)

Growth Isn't Crying, It's Changing

A man crying in front of you isn't necessarily a sign of depth, evolution, or emotional progress. It might be vulnerability, sure. But it might also be a tantrum in a grown man's skin, a release valve for feelings he never learned to regulate. And just because he breaks down doesn't mean he's about to break through.

Some women… hell, most of us, have been trained to see tears as progress. We've been handed this cultural script that if he cries, it means he cares, it means he gets it, it means he's **trying**. And sure, sometimes that's true. But more often? It just means he's uncomfortable. That he's overwhelmed. That he's hitting his limit and spilling over, not because he's grown, but because he's flooded.

We've been over-functioning so long that the first time he shows **anything** that looks like a breakthrough, we cling to it like a life raft in a storm. He finally said he's sorry. He finally admitted he's struggling. He finally cracked open. And our hearts leap, because **maybe** now, he's getting it.

But crying isn't the finish line. It's not even the halfway point. **It's just** *noise* **unless it's followed by change.**

Because growth, **real growth,** isn't loud. It's not dramatic. It doesn't show up in big, performative speeches or crocodile tears on your living room floor. Growth is subtle. It's boring. Unpretty. It's a quiet, consistent shift in how someone shows up over time.

- Growth is **pausing** before he reacts.

- Growth is **listening** without weaponizing your words.

- Growth is **not needing a pat on the back** every time he does the bare minimum.

- Growth is **owning his shit**, not just feeling bad about it.

Want to see growth? **Ignore the breakdowns. Track the patterns.**

Check it at 30, 60, 90 days. If it doesn't hold without applause, it isn't growth.

Is he repeating the same mistakes while calling them "slip-ups"? Is he apologizing for the same things he swore he'd stop doing? Is he using his emotions as a get-out-of-jail-free card, expecting you to hand him comfort and cookies every time he feels sad?

Because that's not growth, babe, that's regression dressed up as depth.

And look, you're not cold-hearted cow for wanting more than emotional chaos and high-stakes sob stories. You're not a monster for saying, "Okay, but now what?" after his tenth meltdown over the same issue. You're allowed to ask for **integration**. For accountability. For follow-through. That doesn't make you cruel, it makes you **clear**.

Here's something no one tells you: **feelings are not currency.** You don't owe someone your forgiveness, your time, or your energy just because they cried. Especially when their tears come only **after** they've hurt you, and never **before** they chose the behavior that did.

You've probably been conditioned to feel guilty for expecting results. To think that demanding real change makes you mean, or "too hard on him," or "uncompassionate." But expecting change is not cruelty. It's discernment.

You've cried, too—haven't you? Probably behind closed doors. Probably into your pillow. Probably at 2 a.m. when you realized you were in this thing alone. But no one threw you a parade for your tears. No one called *you* brave for staying and trying and holding it all together.

So don't let a man's emotional performance become your excuse to stay stuck. Don't confuse a moment of release with a lifetime of effort.

Growth is changing. Consistently. Humbly. Quietly.

You're Not Being Mean, You're Being Honest

Let's stop pretending that honesty is an act of war.

It's not. It's not a grenade. It's not you being mean, or dramatic, or emotionally unstable. It's just you (finally) saying what's been sitting on your chest for too long. It's you pulling the curtain back on the performance and asking, *"Are we actually okay? Or have I just been clapping through the show so we don't have to admit it's falling apart?"*

If that feels dangerous, ask yourself: **Who taught you that truth is toxic?**

Probably not out loud. More like in the thousands of micro-lessons you absorbed growing up. Watching the women in your life smile through clenched teeth, smooth everything over, and apologize for having perfectly normal human emotions while the men around them were allowed

to grunt, sulk, rage, check out, or disappear behind a wall of silence…
and still somehow got branded as "good guys."

So if you've spent your relationship carefully adjusting your tone like it's
a volume knob on a fragile stereo, checking the weather of his moods
before you dare speak up, waiting for launch-window timing just to say,
Hey, this thing is hurting me, then yeah… it's going to feel **dangerous** when
you finally drop the act and say it plain.

But that doesn't make you harsh. That makes you **honest**.

Clarity isn't cruelty. Naming a dynamic isn't an attack. Saying what you
need isn't harsh. You've swallowed the truth a thousand times to keep a
peace that wasn't peaceful. **Now say it out loud.**

Somewhere along the way, "kindness" got twisted into "suffer silently."
And you learned to be **palatable**. To deliver your feelings like a waiter
serving bad news with a smile — *"I'm sorry, the kitchen's all out of emotional
reciprocity tonight. Can I interest you in more self-sacrifice instead?"*

And he? He was taught to equate honesty with attack. So, the minute you
stop phrasing everything like a question or soft suggestion, he hears it
like a missile. You say, *"I feel like I'm doing this alone,"* and he hears, *"You're
a failure."* You say, *"I need more support,"* and he responds like you just
called him useless.

That's not on you.

That's a man who never learned the difference between criticism and
accountability. That's someone whose comfort zone is you tiptoeing, and
who has no idea what to do when you stop.

And he might react. Oh, he probably **will** react. He might get defensive. He might guilt-trip. He might accuse you of being mean, cold, or "not the woman I fell in love with," because guess what? The woman he fell in love with may have been bending herself into pretzels to keep everything running smoothly, and now you've stopped.

But that's not a betrayal. That's a **return to self**.

Because protecting his comfort at the expense of your own sanity is not a love story. It's a slow bleed.

So let him squirm. Let him get uncomfortable. Let the silence sit after you've said what you need to say. You do **not** have to chase the conversation and pad it with reassurances like, *"I don't mean to be harsh,"* or *"I know you're trying."* You can just say the thing. And sit in your own stillness while it lands.

Because if the relationship can't survive the **truth**, then it sure as hell couldn't survive the future you were pretending to build together.

Honesty is a filter. It separates what's real from what's rehearsed. It's not always gentle, but it's always **generous**, especially when you've been stuck in emotional small talk for years.

The Difference Between Trying and Stalling

Let's talk about one of the most manipulative, confusing, soul-exhausting little traps that too many women have mistaken for hope: **the illusion of effort**. That perfectly timed apology. That one decent chore done unprompted. That emotional monologue where he looks at you with wet eyes and says, *"I'm really trying."* And for a second… maybe a whole week… you believe it.

Because you want to believe it.

Because **God**, how badly do you want that corner to finally turn.

He says he wants to do better. He says you matter more than anything. He gets misty-eyed when you finally break down from carrying the weight of two people's emotional lives. And maybe, just maybe, he even vacuums the damn lounge room without you asking, and suddenly you're standing there thinking, *"Is this the shift? Is this finally the break-through?"*

And then three days later, it's like nothing happened. The mess is back. The silence is back. The defensive reactions are back. And you're back to wondering if maybe **you** are the one expecting too much.

But listen to me. And I mean **listen** with the full weight of a best friend shaking your shoulders and not letting you look away:

Effort isn't effort if it evaporates when your tears dry.

That's not growth. That's stalling dressed up as sincerity. That's a man who's learned how to perform just enough to keep the door from closing all the way, without actually having to walk through it and stay in the room when it gets uncomfortable.

See, trying and stalling are twins from a distance. They both say the right things. They both make emotional gestures. They both **look** like care. But only one leads to anything changing. And it's not the one that shows up when he's scared you're leaving. It's the one that keeps showing up after you stop chasing, coaching, reminding, and emotionally holding his damn hand.

So how do you tell the difference?

Trying looks like:

- Bringing the issue back up **himself**, without prompting.

- Doing the thing he said he'd do, without fanfare or a parade.

- Sitting in discomfort without turning it into a meltdown.

- Adjusting when he messes up, instead of defending it.

- Listening without weaponizing your tone against you.

Stalling looks like:

- Only moving when you've hit your breaking point.

- Saying *"I'm sorry"* like a reflex, but nothing else shifts.

- Crying or panicking to derail the real conversation.

- Saying *"You're right"* just to end the conflict.

- Using his fear of loss as fuel, not genuine accountability.

Stalling is a loop. It's the circle you've been running in, telling yourself it's a journey because every now and then he **says** he wants to change.

Trying moves. Even if it's slow. Even if it's awkward. Even if it's clunky as hell and you're both relearning how to talk to each other like grownups. Trying creates a new pattern. It builds trust, not just relief. It doesn't erase the past, but it makes the present bearable and the future less terrifying.

And if the only evidence of his effort is the panic he shows when you're halfway out the door? That's not effort. That's **self-preservation**. That's the internal fire alarm going off and him tossing buckets of charm at the smoke until you agree to stay in the burning building.

No, thank you.

If he only **tries** when you might leave, that isn't building. **That's CPR on a corpse he won't bury.**

And look… I get it. You want to believe in him. You love him. You want to be able to say, *"We made it."* But girl, **you** don't make it unless **he** gets real about what making it actually requires. And that means you can't be the one dragging him across the finish line while he waves and smiles and tells people he's working on himself if he's not.

You don't need a lab coat to see the difference between trying and stalling. Here's a snapshot of what **patterns over promises** looks like in real life.

Audrey Did Everything Right, And Still Walked Alone

Audrey was married to a man who had big struggles. Clinical-level mental health stuff. Depression, anxiety, emotional paralysis on repeat. Some days he wouldn't get off the couch. Others, he'd vanish into himself for days like a ghost in his own home.

She didn't bail. She did what good women are trained to do: she poured. She managed the house, the appointments, the moods, the two kids. She gave space, gave grace, gave up sleep, gave everything.

She carried his hurt and her own like twin backpacks, because she believed in him. Because she believed in love. Because she thought if she just held on long enough, showed him enough, sacrificed enough… maybe something would shift.

It didn't.

And when she finally left, it wasn't a dramatic escape or a big middle finger. It was quiet. Calm. Just a woman who had nothing left to give and finally realized that waiting for someone to show up isn't the same as being loved.

And after the divorce?

She tried again. She dated. Intentionally. With hope.

What she found was a sea of men who, while slightly more functional than her ex, were still emotionally MIA. Couldn't follow through. Couldn't plan a date. Couldn't have a real conversation that didn't short-circuit the moment vulnerability entered the chat.

Audrey — hilarious, self-aware fire-cracker Audrey — joked one day, *"Maybe I should just date women. At least they reply to texts and know how to say sorry."*

She laughed. But she wasn't really joking.

What she meant was: *I'm exhausted from always being the one who tries harder.*

What she meant was: *I've had enough of men who only show up when they're scared of losing you, not when they actually want to grow.*

What she meant was: *I've done the test. I've watched. And I've learned that follow-through doesn't lie.*

What this story teaches you

Here's the raw truth Audrey, and so many women like her, learned the hard way:

- **Effort without consistency is just emotional theater.**

- **Follow-through is love in motion.**

- **Stalling feels a hell of a lot like trying if you're not paying attention.**

This Is the Line in the Sand

You've tested. You've waited. You've watched. Now what?

Now we cross the threshold.

Because you've done enough. You've given enough.

And Part 2?

It's about what happens **next**.

PART II:

YOU CAN'T FIX A GROWN-ASS MAN

CHAPTER 4:

LOVING POTENTIAL IS HOW YOU LOSE YOURSELF

The Fantasy That Keeps You Hooked

He Could Be Amazing... Someday

Look, I know you're not dumb. You're reading this, aren't you…

You're smart. You see things clearly. You see his potential so vividly you can almost taste it. The kind, stable, self-aware guy who's hiding under layers of emotional mess and avoidance. You know exactly what he could be, **if only he got his shit together**.

And the thing is, it's not even a stretch. He's charming enough, funny enough, smart enough. He has these flashes of brilliance and depth that genuinely take your breath away. Moments when you think, "There he is. That's the man I could build a life with."

Here's the gut punch. Those moments are just that… **moments**. Brief glimpses of what he could become, not the consistent reality of who he is right now.

And you keep telling yourself:

- **Someday**, he'll figure it out.

- **Someday**, he'll be ready to commit, communicate clearly, handle conflict without melting down.

- **Someday**, he'll learn how to actually plan a damn date without needing you to hold his hand through the entire thing.

But someday never arrives, does it?

The brutal truth is, you're dating, or married to, **his potential**. You're investing your time, your energy, your sanity, into a fantasy version of him. A version he's shown no concrete signs of becoming anytime soon. Because becoming that guy? It takes effort. Painful self-awareness. Actual change. And why would he bother with any of that uncomfortable work if you're already right here, loving him exactly as he is (and exactly as he isn't)?

I get it, truly. Walking away from potential feels terrifying. It feels like giving up. Like maybe you didn't try hard enough. Like maybe he was right around the corner from being the man you dreamed he could be, and you missed it because you gave up too soon.

How many corners have you already turned… how many second chances handed out like Halloween candy… how many excuses made for a man who can make his own.

Potential is seductive. **Hope isn't the problem. The lie is thinking hope replaces evidence.** You start saying things like, *"He's just going through a rough patch,"* or *"Things will get better when..."* or *"He really is trying... deep down."*

But you know what "trying deep down" usually means? Not actually trying at all.

And here's what you're missing in this endless loop of potential-chasing: **your own damn potential.** Your chance to be with someone who matches your effort, someone who shows up consistently, someone who doesn't require a constant emotional cheerleader, coach, and crisis manager. You deserve someone who isn't an unfinished DIY project.

Because love isn't about loving what someone could be, it's about seeing clearly who they are **today** and asking yourself, *"Is this enough for me?"*

If it isn't… and let's be real, it probably hasn't been for a long time… it's okay to stop waiting on "someday." Because while you're busy waiting, you're missing out on what you could be building right now.

Someday isn't a day. Potential doesn't hold you when life falls apart. You deserve a relationship built on reality, not maybe.

You can't build a life with "maybe someday." But you can build one by choosing what's real, even if that means walking away from the amazing man he might never actually become.

Because here's the truth you probably know deep in your bones but hate admitting: His potential is beautiful. But **your life** is way too short to spend waiting for it.

Ready for the simplest test… **are you loving a person, or an idea.**

You're Dating the Potential, Not the Person

It always starts with the story in your head.

He has depth. He's just guarded He's sweet, he's smart, he's been through so much. If he could just sort out that one thing (his communication, his follow-through, his unresolved trauma, his complete inability to show up emotionally), then he'd be the partner of your dreams.

But here's the catch: **you're not actually in love with him.**

You're in love with who he **could be**. Who he **would be**, if he healed.

Who he **should be**, if he tried.

And that version of him? That's the guy who texts back. Who remembers things. Who plans ahead. Who listens. Who doesn't get defensive when you speak your truth. That man lives in your **mind**, not your relationship.

Meanwhile, the real-life version of him is sitting on the couch dodging accountability like it's a contact sport.

This is how women get stuck: not because they're weak, but because they're hopeful. Hopeful that their patience, love, and effort will pull the man out of his emotional hiding place and magically turn him into someone else.

You become a full-time emotional investor, building a relationship portfolio based on imagination. But you're getting no return, except fatigue, confusion, and that gnawing feeling that something's **off**, even though you keep telling yourself it's just a "rough patch."

Let's break it down:

- **The person** avoids difficult conversations.

- **The potential** just "needs time to open up."

- **The person** doesn't follow through on promises.

- **The potential** is "just under a lot of pressure right now."

- **The person** leaves you feeling unseen.

- **The potential would** see you, if he weren't so "distracted" by work/family/life.

Do you see what's happening?

You're building a whole emotional defense team for a man who wouldn't show up to court. You're protecting someone who hasn't proven they're willing (or able) to protect **you**.

And let's be honest: some of the attraction is the challenge itself. You start to feel like if **you** can get through to him, if **you** can be the one he finally changes for, it'll mean something. It'll prove your worth.

But your worth isn't a prize he gets once he levels up. And his growth isn't your reward for sticking it out.

Here's what makes this so messy: he's not **terrible**. He has good moments. He says the right things sometimes. He shows just enough effort to keep your hope alive, but never enough to give you peace of mind.

It's breadcrumbing, not bonding.

And those crumbs? You've been living on them. Convincing yourself it's a meal.

You deserve better than that. Not because you're perfect, but because you're **present**. You're doing the work. You're self-aware. You're emotionally available. You're out here trying to build something real while he's still fumbling with the box of parts and pretending to read the instructions.

It's time to ask yourself the question no one wants to face:

If he never changed… ever… would you still want this relationship?

If the answer is no, then stop dating the man in your head.

He doesn't exist.

The person in front of you is the only version that matters. And if you keep squinting to see the potential, you'll miss the reality screaming back at you.

You don't need another promise. You need proof. You don't need a fixer-upper. You need a f*cking partner. You don't need to keep holding space for his evolution while neglecting your own.

Set the fantasy down. **Look at the person. Choose from reality.**

Backed by Science

Intermittent rewards create the strongest attachment. When good moments arrive unpredictably, the brain overvalues them and keeps investing. Add the **sunk cost fallacy** and you'll stay longer simply because you've already stayed long.

Translation: your attachment isn't proof it's right. **It's proof the schedule hooked you.**

You're Not Delusional, But Hopeful. And Tired.

This whole thing didn't happen because you're crazy, or blind or stupid. You're not any of that.

What you are is hopeful. **Painfully** hopeful. Because women like you — emotionally intelligent, high-capacity, deeply loving women — **don't**

give up easily. You see the best in people. You hold on a little longer than you should. You want to believe that effort, loyalty, and love can pull someone into their potential.

It's easier to call yourself delusional than admit you've been running on **hope fumes**.

But delusional? No. You saw **something**. You just kept seeing it long after it stopped showing up in reality.

Hope is beautiful. But hope mixed with emotional exhaustion turns into a trap. You're not just tired from life, you're tired from constantly trying to bridge the gap between what your relationship **is** and what you know it **could** be.

You keep thinking:

- Maybe I'm expecting too much.

- Maybe relationships just aren't supposed to feel easy.

- Maybe I need to be more patient, more understanding, more flexible.

And you know what? **Your standards aren't too high. Your bullshit threshold is.**

You're exhausted not because you want too much, but because you've been over-functioning, over-analyzing, and overcompensating for someone who's underdelivering. Repeatedly.

And the worst part isn't even the disappointment.

It's the gaslighting of your own intuition.

You've had those gut moments. You've seen the patterns. You've felt the "off" energy. But you second-guess yourself. You tell yourself to wait it out. That you just need to communicate better. That you're "just in your head."

No. You're in your heart, and it's **worn out to pieces**.

So no, you're not delusional. You're just trying to make sense of someone who's inconsistent, emotionally unavailable, and charming just enough to keep you wondering if the real problem is **you**.

But deep down, you know the truth.

You know you've been compromising more than growing.

You know you've been holding this relationship together with emotional duct tape.

That kind of tired doesn't come from work. It comes from trying to carry something you were never meant to hold alone.

So, no. You're not crazy. **You're tired of carrying a two-person job.**

The Nurturer Trap

You Were Raised to Pour. He Was Raised to Receive.

This didn't start with him. Not really.

It started way before him, with the blueprint you were handed long before you ever dated, before you even understood what relationships really were. Because you were taught early, in quiet, subtle, soul-shaping ways, that being a good girl meant being good **for** everyone else.

You were raised to notice. To accommodate. To be thoughtful without being asked. You were the one who remembered birthdays, kept peace during arguments, said sorry first, and somehow always ended up carrying the feelings of an entire room like emotional luggage strapped to your back, because it was easier to carry it than to watch people fall apart.

Meanwhile, the boys? They were taught from a different textbook. They got to stomp and sulk and shut down, and people just shrugged and said, *"That's how boys are."* They weren't called too much. They weren't expected to babysit the emotions of everyone around them. They were allowed to just… exist.

So, by the time you two meet — him with his unexamined entitlement to ease, and you with your well-worn habit of hyper-functioning — you're already halfway into the pattern. Neither of you notices the imbalance at first. It feels normal. Familiar. Like a script you both memorized in different childhood households.

And it works, for a while. Until one day it doesn't.

Until you realize that you've become the thermostat for the entire emotional climate of the relationship, that you're constantly scanning, managing, softening, fixing. That your nervous system is working overtime trying to create harmony while he just... lives in it.

And what stings the most? He doesn't even know you're tired.

Because he's used to women like you. Women who anticipate, soothe, explain. Women who hand out emotional gold stars just for bare-minimum decency. Women who over-function and under-ask.

He doesn't think you're tired. He thinks this is just how you love.

But you know the truth now. You know that this isn't your love language. It's your trauma language. It's what happens when you grow up believing that being lovable means being low-maintenance, grateful, and never, ever a burden.

It's what happens when no one ever taught you that your needs matter just as much as his comfort.

You were trained to **pour**, not receive. So, when you need, when you want, reaching out feels foreign. It feels risky. It feels like a betrayal of everything you've been told makes you "good."

But here's the thing: **You can stop.**

You can stop pouring when your cup is empty. You can stop smiling when your insides are screaming. You can stop tiptoeing around his moods, his triggers, his fragile sense of self, just to keep the peace in a house where you haven't felt peaceful in months.

This isn't you giving up. This is you waking up.

Because if he only shows up when you fall apart, if the only time he pays attention is when you collapse from the weight of carrying everything alone, he's not a partner. He's a passive participant in your burnout.

And no, this doesn't make him a monster. But it does mean you've been managing a relationship on your own, with a man who thinks that not being "as bad as your ex" is the same thing as being a good partner.

He isn't a monster. **But he is responsible. So are you.** Responsible for stopping a pattern that feeds on silence.

You deserve **reciprocity**. Because you are a whole, breathing human being.

So, the next time you feel guilty for needing too much, or not "being there" like you used to be, remember this:

You were raised to pour. You're allowed to stop.

When Love Becomes a Project Plan

You didn't fall in love thinking, *"Ah yes, this man is clearly an unfinished IKEA shelf of a human, I will assemble him with love, patience, and a tiny emotional Allen key."*

But if you're honest?

You've got a whole-ass project plan running in your head. Tabs open. Post-its on your soul. **Emotional Gantt charts** for his moods. You know when to push. When to pull back. When to phrase things just right so he doesn't shut down, lash out, or do that thing where he stares blankly at you like you're speaking ancient Greek instead of simple emotional English.

And somewhere along the way, without meaning to, love stopped being a connection and started being a job. A spreadsheet. A performance dashboard with metrics like:

- Didn't forget anniversary?

- Actually said what he was feeling?

- Didn't storm off mid-convo when I said something mildly uncomfortable?

And each time he meets one of these bare-minimum milestones, you get this strange mix of relief and exhaustion, like a teacher watching a struggling student finally turn in homework after weeks of chasing.

You're not his teacher. You're his partner.

Except now, you're deep in the weeds of fixing, explaining, over-functioning, trying to upgrade his emotional software while pretending you're okay running on fumes. You're loving him the way you manage everything else in your life: like a high-capacity woman who's used to solving problems. And God, you are so good at it. Too good.

So good that he never has to stretch. So good that he gets to stay comfortable while you bend yourself into a pretzel trying to make this relationship "work."

And the hardest part? You've convinced yourself that this is what love looks like. That if you just love him **right**, he'll finally become the man you see inside him. The one with all that potential.

Girl… that's not love. That's emotional gentrification.

That's you investing in his future while yours sits on hold.

Because if he's not building it with you, if he's just coasting while you sweat, it's not a partnership. It's a renovation project. And you're the unpaid contractor working overtime, fixing up someone else's foundation with no guarantee they'll ever move in emotionally.

Here's what no one tells you when you're busy giving second, third, fourth chances:

You can't love someone into emotional adulthood. You can't cry, sex, support, or therapize someone into readiness. That part? It's their job.

And when you take it on, when you become the relationship architect while they just sort of show up and "mean well," you create something really confusing. He doesn't know when you're going to be the loving girlfriend or the low-key life coach. And you? You start to resent the whole damn thing but feel guilty for resenting it, because "he's trying."

Except he's not. Not really. He's reacting. Reacting to your nudges, your strategies, your perfectly timed pep talks. He's tweaking just enough to keep you from walking, not changing enough to meet you where you actually live.

And you're tired.

Not just "busy tired."

I mean that soul-worn, dead-eyed, please-don't-make-me-have-another-conversation tired.

Because no matter how many late-night "I just want us to get better" talks you've had, no matter how many articles you've sent or breakdowns you've endured quietly, hoping it might finally land — nothing changes. Or if it does, it boomerangs right back to the old baseline like a rubber band that snapped the second you let go of the tension.

And here's the part that really messes you up:

You start to feel *guilty* for wanting out. You start thinking, "But I've already put so much work in," like love is a sunken cost you can't walk away from.

Love isn't a loyalty test. **Effort without evolution is a trap.**

So put the clipboard down.

Shut the project file.

Step out of the job you were never hired for.

And ask yourself the question you've been avoiding every time you re-download hope… that same terrifying question I've already planted for you:

If this is who he stays… can you live with that?

And if the answer even flickers toward "no," it's time to stop managing his potential and start managing your peace.

You don't need to flip another man-shaped fixer-upper.

You need someone who walks into the damn house ready to co-own it with you.

The Heartbreak of Trying to Grow Someone Who Won't Water Himself

There's a specific kind of heartbreak that doesn't come from betrayal or screaming fights or dramatic walkouts. It comes from the slow, aching realization that you've been pouring your love into someone like sunlight on a rock, begging it to bloom.

You saw the potential. You saw the soul underneath the shutdowns and silences. You saw the moments of softness, the glimpses of depth, the tiny shards of effort that made you believe, deep down, that he could grow into something solid and grounded and whole. And because you're a builder, a nurturer, a deeply feeling woman who knows how to pour and pour and pour, you decided to invest. To love harder. To guide him toward his own evolution. To become the emotional scaffolding he never had.

But here's the part that lands like a gut punch after years of trying: **he has to want it for himself.**

You can't will someone into growth. You can't love them into maturity. You can't drag them across the finish line of their own emotional development if they're determined to sit down halfway and say it's too hard. And you sure as hell can't keep watering a garden that never had roots in the first place.

Because what you're doing, when you stay in that loop of "he'll get there eventually," is breaking your own heart in the softest, cruelest way possible — by hoping just long enough to stay stuck.

And the pain is confusing. It doesn't come with clarity. It comes with fog. Because he's not a monster. He's not abusive. He might even be kind, sweet, charming, loving in his way. But his way? It's not enough. Not for you. Not for the life you want. Not for the woman you are becoming.

And that hurts.

It hurts because you didn't love carelessly. You gave your whole heart. You tried. You compromised. You adapted your needs so they would fit inside the small emotional container he offered, convincing yourself that asking for more would make you selfish or ungrateful. You shrunk slowly and carefully, the way women do when they're trying not to make anyone uncomfortable. And you called it patience. You called it love. You called it growth.

But what it was… what it actually was… was heartbreak in slow motion.

Because while you were nurturing, planning, hoping, and doing all the right things, **he was standing still.** Maybe not maliciously. Maybe not even consciously. But still. And every time you reached out to pull him forward, all you got was **resistance posing as effort.** Promises without follow-through. Emotion without endurance. A thousand tiny moments of hope with no structure to hold them.

And that's the thing no one warns you about — **how hard it is to leave someone who isn't horrible,** just unready. How easy it is to confuse potential with progress. How devastating it is to realize that love alone isn't enough if you're the only one doing the growing.

You didn't fail.

You didn't love wrong.

You finally realized… no matter how much sunlight, water, care you give, **if he won't grow roots, nothing grows.**

And you? You deserve a partner who meets you in the soil. Who gets dirty with you. Who waters himself. Who knows that growth isn't optional, it's essential.

So, if he didn't pick up that ball, let go. Not because you didn't care, but because you cared enough to know that staying would only keep breaking something that should have been built together.

This is not weakness.

This is wisdom.

You deserve a partner who meets you in the soil, gets dirty, **waters himself**, and knows growth isn't optional.

When they ask why you left, you don't need a villain. Say this: *"I was trying to grow something with a man who never picked up the watering can."*

Takeaway

If You're Dating Potential:

• Hope isn't data.

• Intermittent effort isn't growth.

• Follow-through is the metric.

• Caretaking kills chemistry.

• Love without evolution is a trap.

Choose what's real.

Next up: what safe actually feels like… and how to tell if it's even possible here.

You're Not His Safe Space If He's Your War Zone

What Real Safety Looks Like (and What It Doesn't)

There is one thing I'm begging you to carve in your mind: **emotional safety is not walking on eggshells to "keep the peace."** If you're filtering every sentence through a mental PR department, avoiding hard topics so he doesn't spiral or sulk or snap, that's not emotional safety. That's emotional containment. Of you.

And girl, that shit's exhausting.

You want to know what actual, soul-deep, exhale-into-the-car-seat safety looks like? It looks like being able to say, *I'm not okay*, and not having to brace for the emotional fallout. It looks like being allowed to be a whole human without him flipping it into a guilt trip about how your tone made him feel like trash. It looks like knowing you can have a bad day without being made to pay for it later.

It doesn't mean no arguments. **It means the hard stuff isn't hazardous**, even when he's tired or annoyed.

Safety isn't perfection, it's pattern. It's how he reacts over time, not once on a good day when he's well fed, well slept, and the sun is shining. It's what he does when he's uncomfortable and still manages to treat you like a person, not a problem.

Let's talk about what emotional safety is not, because some of you are out here thinking, *"Well, he doesn't yell, so I guess I'm fine."*

No.

If you:

- Rehearse conversations like you're prepping a hostage negotiation…

- Get anxious before bringing up anything emotional…

- Feel like your moods are "too much" while his get catered to like a sick puppy…

- Say *I feel hurt* and get back *Well, here you go again…*

You are not safe.

And look, I bet you're thinking, *He means well. He's trying. He's just not used to this kind of communication.* Sure. But even if he's not yelling, even if he's not cruel, even if he "doesn't mean to," if you don't feel safe being fully you in your own relationship, **it isn't working.**

If his feelings always take center stage and yours are an inconvenience to be managed, **you're not safe. You're performing.**

And performing, babe, is exhausting. It turns you into the translator, the peacekeeper, the emotional mule. You say things gently so he doesn't take them the wrong way. You hold things in because you're afraid of how he'll take it. You water yourself down so he can feel tall.

Meanwhile, **you're the one shrinking.** You're the one lonely in the middle of the relationship.

I know it's tempting to say, *Nobody's perfect,* and brush this off like it's just a communication mismatch. But this isn't about perfection. **It's about capacity.** Can he stay in the room when it's hard? Can he sit in discomfort without lashing out or shutting down? **Can you be angry, messy, uncertain… and still loved?**

That's safety.

It's not always pretty. But it's steady. You don't have to second-guess every sentence. You don't have to think, *How do I say this so he doesn't spiral?* You don't have to be less just to be heard.

Because here's the truth: **you weren't made to be agreeable. You were made to be whole.**

You deserve a relationship where you can speak freely, cry loudly, laugh at the wrong time, and say, *That hurt*, without it turning into a referendum on your character.

So, if you're constantly managing his feelings, cushioning your truth, and checking yourself to keep things "calm," it's not calm. **It's suppression.** And it won't work long term.

Without safety, love turns into labor. And no matter how many kisses or cuddles you get in between, **you're still carrying a relationship that should be walking beside you.**

Because when safety costs you self-expression, **you're not safe, you're staged.**

So, let's stop calling survival "maturity."

You don't have to earn your right to exist.

You don't have to audition for peace.

You get to be all of you… and still feel loved.

Why You Always Apologizing Means No One Is Safe

If you've been in survival mode long enough (and girl, I know you have), apologies probably roll out of your mouth like breath. Not because you've done anything wrong, but because somewhere along the line your brain learned your honesty is dangerous. That your feelings are disruptive. That if you speak up without softening the blow, you'll ruin everything.

So, you say it.

Sorry I brought that up.

Sorry, I'm probably overreacting.

Sorry for how that sounded.

You apologize for existing in full volume, for needing space, truth, respect. You apologize before he can even react, because you've learned it's safer to preemptively kneel than risk standing tall and watching the room shake.

Every time you do it, even when it feels small, even when it's just a reflex, you send both of you a message: **my truth is a problem.**

Say it enough times and guess what happens? **He believes it too.** Your emotions become overreactions. Your boundaries become unreasonable. Your needs become burdens. And you start folding yourself smaller and smaller to take up less space in the relationship you're supposed to thrive in.

Apologizing for your truth doesn't make things safer. **It makes you invisible.**

It tells him, *Your comfort matters more than my clarity.*

It tells your nervous system, *We're not allowed to be real here.*

It builds a relationship where peace means silence and connection means suppression.

Let's be really clear — **this is not what love looks like.** Love isn't filtering yourself so he never feels discomfort. Love isn't swallowing your pain because he gets defensive. Love isn't protecting his ego while yours shatters every time you say *sorry* when you meant **enough**.

When you keep apologizing for things that aren't wrong, you train both of you to believe emotional regulation is your job.

It isn't.

You are not his babysitter, PR manager, guilt sponge, or damage-control department. You are not here to wrap yourself in bubble wrap so he doesn't stub his ego every time you say something true.

And I know how scary it feels to stop apologizing. You've probably been doing it since childhood. You learned that being pleasant and non-threatening makes you easier to love. You learned that being good means being agreeable. You learned that saying how you really feel makes people explode… or leave.

Listen to me: **if your honesty burns the house down, the house was already on fire.** Every reflexive *sorry* teaches your nervous system that truth equals danger. A relationship that can't handle your truth doesn't deserve your silence.

Yes, when you stop apologizing, things will shift. He might lash out. He might pout. He might act like you've changed. And you have. You finally stopped performing safety at the expense of your own.

That's not cruelty. **That's clarity.**

That's what it looks like to reclaim your right to speak plainly. To feel without guilt. To ask for what you need without groveling.

And him? He's allowed to squirm. **Let him.** Let him sit with the discomfort of not being your emotional sun. Let him feel what it's like to be in a relationship with a whole human who doesn't twist herself into knots just to keep him comfortable.

If he can't handle that, **he's not safe.** Not for you. Not for anyone.

You've been the safe one for everyone else long enough. **Now it's your turn.**

Accountability Without Blame

You're Not Asking for Perfection, You're Asking for Partnership

There's a difference between being emotionally incapable and being emotionally unmotivated. One is a skill gap. The other is convenience. **The first can be learned. The second can't, because it doesn't want to.**

And a lot of men? **They're Ray Barone with a smartphone** — pretending they don't know how to schedule a doctor's appointment, send a thoughtful text, or initiate a real conversation unless you spoon-feed the blueprint.

You've heard him say, *I'm just not good at that kind of stuff.* Translation: *I've never had to try, because someone like you always handled it for me.*

He's not helpless. He's been conditioned to believe emotional labor is optional for him and mandatory for you.

You are not dramatic, difficult, hard to love, or some exhausting human Rubik's cube. You're just sick of being in a relationship where **basic decency** is treated like a premium feature you forgot to unlock. You're not looking for a mythical, emotionally advanced man-god who reads your mind. You're asking for a man who shows up consistently — present, aware, willing to carry some of the load without being dragged, begged, or bribed.

You're asking for the baseline: **effort, thoughtfulness, growth, presence.**

And still… it's somehow too much.

God forbid you say, *I need help*, without a preamble proving it isn't a personal attack or ingratitude for that one time last year he bought servo flowers. It's wild how low the bar is. **You're giving therapy-level insight, emotional forecasting, and logistical planning** while he gets praised for not emotionally imploding during a mildly stressful day.

Most of us don't even ask for half of what we need. We dilute it. We delay it. We soften and shrink it to make it easier to swallow. We play the good partner, the understanding one, the *I'll just handle it, he's overwhelmed* martyr. Then when we finally ask, calmly and clearly, it's treated like an unfair burden.

Ask him to help with the emotional labor? *You're too sensitive.*

Ask him to handle his own schedule? *Why are you so controlling?*

Ask him to initiate, plan something, stop making you feel like the whole relationship lives in your hands? *Nothing I do is ever enough.*

Sound familiar?

He's not broken or incapable. **He's used to being Ray Barone — for**getting everything, doing nothing, being cute about it, and laughing it off like it's endearing. Guess what? You're not living in a sitcom, and you don't get paid to be the straight woman to his mess.

Meanwhile, you're clapping like a seal every time he wipes the bench or makes a dentist appointment unprompted. You're so hungry for partnership that you're praising crumbs and trying to convince yourself they taste like cake.

If we're being blunt: this isn't about expecting perfection. **It's about expecting participation.** Expect to be met — not worshipped, not served, **met** — by someone who understands that being in a relationship means showing up for more than the fun parts.

It means stepping up when things are uncomfortable.

It means taking initiative when you're tired.

It means not turning every feedback session into a hostage negotiation where you're tied to the emotional chair explaining why his silence makes you feel invisible while he stares at the floor waiting for the storm to pass.

You're not asking for flawless communication. **You're asking for someone who doesn't treat feedback like a personal attack.**

You're not asking him to never mess up. **You're asking him to own it when he does.**

If that sounds radical to him, maybe he's not used to being in a relationship — maybe he's used to being cared for. **Which isn't the same thing.**

Here's the truth: a man who wants to grow hears your needs as an invitation. A man who doesn't hears them as a complaint. That difference is everything.

So no, you're not asking for too much. You're finally asking for what you always deserved and stopped pretending was optional.

If that makes him uncomfortable, **let him sit with it.** Let him feel what it means to be a partner, not a passenger. Because if he needs you small to feel big, if he needs you silent to feel secure, what you have isn't partnership. **It's proximity.**

And proximity doesn't carry the weight.

You do.

So, drop it. **Speak it. Demand it.** You're not here to be agreeable; you're here to be seen. **And if he can't, move.**

How to Hold Space Without Holding the Entire Emotional Load

You don't need a lesson in empathy. You've been running an all-inclusive emotional resort for years. You've held space so beautifully, so endlessly, your relationship should come with a guest check-in form and a minibar charge. You've listened without judgment. You've validated without being asked. You've been patient through every mood swing, work meltdown, identity crisis, childhood wound resurface, and emotional hangover… and still managed to fold the laundry and text back in under two minutes with a *You got this, babe.*

Some of that is love. It's you being the deeply feeling, big-hearted human you are.

But some of it is **you dissolving into the background of your own life** because you were busy absorbing his. It's you shapeshifting into whatever version of yourself made the least waves, because keeping him stable felt more important than staying whole. That's not "holding space." **That's being a shock absorber.** That's drowning politely while smiling and pretending the view is lovely.

There is a massive difference between being there for someone and being their emotional cleanup crew. One is supportive. **The other is self-erasure.**

It felt natural at first. Familiar. He had big feelings? You were there. He was stressed? You found the words. He needed time, space, softness? You folded smaller to fit what he needed. Meanwhile, you cried in the shower and made deals with your own exhaustion.

Because love was sold to you as endurance, not reciprocity. As loyalty. As ride-or-die. But in reality, you weren't standing by him. **You were carrying him.** Dragging the entire weight of the relationship like a backpack full of bricks no one even acknowledged you were holding.

You weren't thriving. **You were bracing.**

So, let's make the distinction real clear. **Holding space** means you show up, you listen, you let him feel his feelings without rushing to make them prettier. You sit next to him in his mess without taking it on like it's your full-time job to fix it. The second you start editing yourself, shrinking needs, monitoring tone, withholding truth, or walking on eggshells to avoid triggering his shame spiral? That's not holding space anymore. **That's becoming emotional furniture.**

You get so convenient he forgets you're a person. A person with limits. A person who is tired of holding everyone together while no one asks, *How are you doing with all of this?*

Here's what it can look like instead: when he's spiraling, you can sit with him, but you don't have to climb in. You can say, *I see you*, without adding, *Here, let me carry this for you.* You can be present without becoming the scaffolding that holds his world together while yours quietly crumbles.

And when it's your turn to need something, to cry, to be scared or snappy or fragile, **you let him hold you.** You let him sit in the discomfort of your truth without softening it for his ego. You speak up without circling the runway for twenty minutes to make sure he doesn't take it the wrong way. If he flinches at your honesty, if he disappears emotionally the second you stop being endlessly available for his needs, what you have isn't a partnership. **It's a codependent performance with you cast in every lead role.**

You're allowed to be generous. You're allowed to be soft. **Not at the cost of becoming invisible.** If the only version of you that gets love is the version that stays silent, soothing, endlessly composed, then what he loves isn't you. **It's what you do for him.**

Support is shared. Servitude isn't.

That's not space. **That's a service.** And you're not in the business of emotional catering anymore.

You're building something mutual, grounded, real. The only way to do that is to stop being his emotional first responder and start being your own.

Emotional Safety Doesn't Mean Silence, It Means Truth Without Punishment

You didn't become quiet because you had nothing to say. You became quiet because experience taught you that saying it came with a cost your nervous system decided wasn't worth paying. You learned that voicing a boundary might earn you an eye roll or a blow-up. That saying, *I'm hurt*, could be met with silence, deflection, defensiveness, or worse, punishment so subtle it left you questioning whether speaking up had been the real problem all along. So, you softened. You delayed. You swallowed it down and convinced yourself maybe it wasn't a big deal.

But here's what no one teaches us, what takes years of inner depletion to understand: **emotional safety isn't the absence of conflict.** It isn't two people smiling politely and avoiding hard conversations until the air gets so thick with unspoken stuff you could slice it with a butter knife. It isn't keeping everything "nice" so he doesn't spiral, or timing your truth for when he's in the right mood, had enough sleep, isn't hungry, isn't stressed, isn't watching the game, and hasn't had "a long day."

Emotional safety is the ability to bring up the hard stuff — raw, real, messy — and know it won't be used against you. It's the ability to say, *I'm not okay*, without being met with a sulk or a shutdown or a guilt trip about how hard his week has been too. It's being able to sit in tension without scrambling to fix it first. It's not choosing between honesty and harmony because your relationship can handle both.

The lie women get sold is that we're too sensitive, too demanding, too dramatic. That good relationships don't fight. That good partners are easygoing. That if you were really mature and grateful, you'd let it slide. So, you do. Again and again… until one day you realize you haven't said a real thing in weeks. You've become so fluent in emotional suppression that you second-guess every instinct before it forms a sentence. **Your truth lives under your tongue like a secret you don't feel entitled to anymore.**

The saddest part? He might think everything's fine. Your silence doesn't look like a problem to someone who benefits from it. He thinks the absence of feedback means satisfaction. He assumes no news is good news. What it really is — what it's always been — is **you disappearing** to keep the peace. Your peace. His peace. Everyone's peace but your own.

So, here's what emotional safety actually looks like: being able to say, *I need more*, without rehearsing it fifty times. Saying, *That hurt*, and not spending the next hour managing his hurt feelings about your hurt feelings. Knowing you can bring something uncomfortable to the table without the whole relationship wobbling like it's held together by eggshells and hope.

If you don't have that — if you're afraid any moment of honesty will be twisted, punished, or ignored — then you don't have safety. **You have performance.** You have emotional labor misbranded as maturity. You have a dynamic where your truth is treated as a threat, not a gift.

Punishment isn't always loud. Sometimes it's the cold shoulder. The three-day mood. The way he stops touching you. The way he acts like your boundary is a betrayal. The way you start walking around your own relationship like a visitor who doesn't want to overstay her welcome. And then that becomes normal. You stop speaking altogether. You become the version of you he can tolerate. She's agreeable. She's quiet. She never rocks the boat. **She's slowly suffocating.**

So let's be clear: **love that requires your silence isn't love.** It's convenience. It's emotional management. It's building your identity around someone else's capacity to handle truth. If it's been a while since you felt heard — not just listened to, **heard** — it's time to stop blaming your delivery and start looking at the delivery system.

You are not too much for wanting to be real. You are not dramatic for wanting to be heard without paying for it in guilt and tension. You are not the problem just because your honesty isn't convenient.

If you have to lie, sugarcoat, tiptoe, hold your breath just to feel safe, maybe it isn't love you're preserving.

Maybe it's the illusion of it.

How to Talk About Hard Things Without Tiptoeing or Torching It

The hardest part isn't knowing what you feel. It's figuring out how to say it without setting off a full-blown emotional house fire.

You've had those internal panic meetings, pacing the living room, replaying the same sentence fifteen different ways. You want to be honest but not too blunt. Clear but not cold. Emotional but not dramatic. So you water it down until it barely tastes like truth, then serve it with a side of guilt and a *please don't get defensive* tone that makes your stomach churn.

Half the time, you're still met with defensiveness or shutdowns. You walk away thinking, *Maybe I should've said it differently… again.*

Girl. Stop. Seriously. **Your voice isn't the problem. His capacity is.** You don't have to yell. You don't have to shrink. You don't have to rehearse your pain like it's a TED Talk with a fragile audience. There's a third way: firm, grounded, human. Truth-telling that doesn't torch the room, but lights up what needs to be seen.

Say it clean, then stop talking.

I'm bringing this up because I care about us. I can't carry this alone anymore.

If he spirals: *This is why I hesitate to speak up.* Then let silence do its job.

If he shuts down the second it's hard… if he flips it into blame, cries victim, or makes it all about your delivery… if he treats your honesty like a bomb instead of a bridge… then no matter how soft you speak or how carefully you package your truth, it will never land. **Not because you're harsh, but because he isn't listening unless it flatters him.**

If that's the case, it isn't a conversation. **It's a performance.** Emotional maturity is revealed in reactions.

So, stop editing your truth to fit his comfort zone. **Start speaking like a woman who knows she deserves to be heard** — not just when it's easy, but especially when it's not.

CHAPTER 5:

GIVE HIM A FAIR CHANCE TO GROW

Stop Fixing, Start Watching

You've already felt it in your bones… that tiny shift where your hands stop hovering over everything, where your mouth closes around one more reminder, where you let the moment breathe instead of rushing in with a solution. Good. That was the warm-up. Now we take it further.

For a long time you made it look easy. You anticipated before anyone asked, you absorbed before anyone noticed, you kept the wheels greased so well the machine seemed frictionless. Which meant he got to believe there was no friction. You celebrated his small wins like confetti, you swallowed your own exhaustion like vitamins, and you told yourself this is what strong women do… they hold it together. **But strength that erases you isn't strength, it's self-abandonment dressed as competence.**

Here's the experiment. You stop fixing. You stop narrating. You stop spoon-feeding the exact words, times, steps, tone, timing. You let the bin overflow for a day. You let the birthday card remain unsent. You let the plan he promised to handle exist in its natural habitat… reality. And you watch.

Not with a clipboard and a grade sheet. With your eyes open and your energy pulled back into your own body. **Observation is not cruelty, it's clarity.** Because every time you warn him or coach him, you're not measuring his growth, you're measuring your choreography. You're seeing a man respond to cues, not initiate from care. That's why the effort always fades when you stop prompting. It was never his rhythm. It was yours.

So you don't announce this shift. You don't sit him down for a heartfelt press conference. You don't say *I'm doing a thing where I step back so I can assess our dynamic fairly.* The second you declare the audit, he'll perform for the audit. What you want is his baseline, the uncoached version, the default setting when nobody is handing him lines. **Who is he when you are not the glue.**

It will feel wrong at first. Your nervous system is used to sprinting. You'll see the drop coming and your whole body will lean forward to catch it. Breathe. Let it fall. Let the discomfort do the teaching you've been trying to do with words. If the bill incurs a late fee, it incurs a late fee. If the dinner doesn't get booked, it doesn't get booked. If he asks why you didn't remind him, you don't deliver a lecture; you deliver truth, simple and clean: *I can't carry all of it. I'm watching what happens when I don't.*

What you're watching for isn't a grand gesture, because those are cheap and loud and short-lived. You're watching for quiet initiative. For him noticing the gap and moving toward it without applause. For follow-through that repeats often enough to feel like a new pattern, not a panic spike. **Change is boring up close. That's how you know it's real.**

And if nothing happens… if your absence is treated like freedom instead of feedback, if he coasts until you break and then calls your boundary *distant* or *cold*, that's data too. Not a scandal, not a headline, just a fact about capacity and willingness. You don't have to argue with facts. You don't have to dress them up or down. You just have to see them and decide what you're building your life on.

So, this is the invitation to yourself: step out of the role of fixer and back into the role of witness. Let the room get quiet enough to hear what the relationship sounds like without your constant hum of labor. **If he rises, you'll see it. If he doesn't, you'll feel it.** Either way, you stop guessing. You stop overexplaining. You stop auditioning for support you've already earned by existing.

Say less. Do less. Watch more.

Your clarity is coming.

Can He Be Called In Without Falling Apart?

There's a world of difference between calling someone out and calling them in. One is about shame and spectacle, public correction and ego bruises. The other is about care. It's relational. It's quiet, steady, and rooted in the hope that this connection can be stronger, if we're both willing to look at where it's breaking down. Calling someone in doesn't mean you're trying to win a fight. It means you believe the relationship is worth repairing.

But even that soft, considered approach, **even the gentlest** *"Hey, can we talk about something that's been weighing on me?",* can turn into a hostage negotiation if the man on the receiving end has the emotional resilience of a houseplant left in a dark room for too long.

You're not even criticizing. You're just sharing. You say, "I've been feeling a little overwhelmed lately," and suddenly he's shut down, sulking, or catastrophizing about how he's "never enough." You say, "I need more support," and he doesn't ask what you mean — he spirals. Into guilt, into silence, into defensiveness so thick you can't even see the original issue anymore. Now you're not discussing your needs. You're managing **his** reaction to your needs. You're walking on eggshells **inside your own vulnerability.**

And maybe you've convinced yourself that he's just sensitive. That he's trying. That he's never had someone really talk to him this way before. Maybe that's even true. But here's the uncomfortable truth you have to face if you're serious about building something healthy: **if a man cannot hold space for your truth without falling apart, he is not ready for the relationship you are trying to build.**

Growth doesn't mean he never gets defensive. It doesn't mean he nods politely through every piece of feedback like a monk who's reached emotional enlightenment. It means he stays. It means he stays in the room, not physically, but emotionally, while you say the hard thing. It means he doesn't immediately start explaining, deflecting, justifying, or flipping the script so the spotlight lands back on his suffering instead of your need.

It means he can feel discomfort without making you pay for it.

Because that's the test, really. Not whether he says the right thing in the moment, but whether he can absorb hard feedback without turning you into the villain for daring to say it. Can he still connect with you, even while hearing that he's let you down? Can he hold that without folding or retaliating?

Because if every tough conversation turns into emotional whiplash, if you walk away feeling like you've just parented a grown man through his own shame spiral, then let's call it what it is: **you're not in a relationship. You're in a caretaking dynamic.** One where your emotional clarity becomes a threat, and his inability to sit in discomfort becomes your responsibility to manage.

And haven't you done enough of that?

So, while you're watching his behavior, while you're pulling back, collecting data, seeing what he does with the space, don't just look for tasks and timelines and whether or not he remembered to put the laundry in.

Watch how he handles being called in. Watch how he receives the truth.

Can he stay connected to you while hearing something that stings?

Can he resist the urge to make it about how hard it is for him to hear, and instead say, *"I hear you. What can I do differently?"*

Can he come back the next day, not with punishment, not with withdrawal, not with guilt trips, but with accountability?

That's not easy. That's not common. That's not instinctive for most people. But **that is emotional adulthood.**

And if he wants to be in a relationship with a woman who sees herself clearly, who speaks the truth and expects to be met in it, then **he has to meet her there.** Not with perfect words. Not with a flawless track record. But with the ability to stay in the room when things get real. With the willingness to listen, to reflect, and to return, not defensive, not sulking, but slightly more aware than he was the day before.

Because that's how you know he's not just trying to perform.

He's learning how to grow.

Silent Audit

When you've carried the emotional load long enough, you become fluent in pre-emptive explanation.

You don't just ask — you cushion. You don't just need — you justify.

Every truth gets padded like fragile cargo before delivery, so it won't explode on impact. That instinct will kick in now too. You'll want to make it **fair**. To tell him, *"I'm not mad, I'm just observing. I need to see what's real without my influence."* Sounds emotionally intelligent, right? Mature, even?

Don't.

The minute you declare your observation, it stops being one. Because now he's performing. Suddenly, he's tidying up his act like a student during a pop quiz. He's volunteering help, asking thoughtful questions, maybe even remembering that you like oat milk — and every move feels rehearsed.

It's not that you don't want improvement. You just want **authentic** improvement. You want to know who he is when nobody's grading him. When there's no emotional leash in your hand. When the bins overflow and the silence stretches and the only cue is life itself.

That's why this is a **silent audit**.

You're not playing games; you're gathering data. When you stop scripting the conversation, you see what he contributes when he's not reading off your teleprompter.

And no, this isn't manipulation.

It's the removal of management.

You're done being the director of his emotional development, the one who highlights every opportunity for growth like a human highlighter pen. If he can't notice the obvious without your stage notes, then what he's offering isn't partnership — it's performance review avoidance.

So, you say nothing.

You step back. You watch how he behaves when no one's prompting him to pass the test.

Strategic Pullback Isn't Punishment, It's Permission

Making Space for His Growth... or His Truth

Someone is going to say you've changed — maybe him, maybe your mother, maybe that one friend who still thinks emotional endurance equals love. They'll say you've become colder, harder, detached, that you're not the same soft, giving version of yourself who used to hold everyone together with a smile and a spreadsheet. And maybe for a second, that accusation will sting. Because part of you still equates care with overextension, and still believes that love means self-erasure.

But remember this: you haven't hardened. **You've clarified**. You've finally stopped confusing endless accommodation with emotional generosity. You've stopped calling self-abandonment compassion.

This isn't punishment. **It's permission** — for him, for you, for the relationship itself — to exist without you acting as the structural support beam that keeps it from collapsing under its own laziness.

And yes, it will look like chaos at first. Because when you've been trimming weeds and watering deserts for years, letting things grow wild will seem reckless. The unpruned parts of him, the cracks in communication, the little places you always patched before they spread — they'll all become visible now. But visibility isn't destruction. It's data. It's the raw, unfiltered truth of what happens when you remove the scaffolding and see if the structure can hold.

This pullback isn't a test to see if he'll chase you or beg you to stay. It's an audit — quiet, unannounced, and deeply revealing. You're not waiting for a grand gesture or a crisis-born apology; you're watching for **baseline behavior**. Who is he when there's no prompt? No script? No applause?

Who is he when the comfort of your constant effort is no longer available to absorb his inertia?

Because that's the moment everything becomes clear — when you stop carrying the emotional weight that made the relationship look balanced.

If he steps up, not just in panic but in sustained presence, then you've learned something hopeful.

But if he waits you out, sulks, blames, or simply enjoys the quiet relief of you doing less — then you've learned something else.

And it's okay if that truth hurts. It's supposed to. It's the sound of false peace cracking open. It's the hum of all those years of self-betrayal finally quieting down. Because when you stop doing the emotional heavy lifting, and the whole structure starts to tremble, you'll realize it was never stable in the first place — it was just you, holding it up with shaking hands and calling it love.

So yes, **let the silence stretch**. Let the space echo. Let the distance breathe.

What fills that silence — his effort, his confusion, his indifference — will tell you more about the future of this relationship than any carefully worded conversation ever could.

And you don't have to explain, justify, or defend your stillness. You just have to hold it. Because silence, when used with intention, isn't cold. It's clarifying. It's the sound of truth emerging from beneath the noise you've been drowning in.

And if anyone tells you you've changed, tell them yes. **You stopped mistaking martyrdom for maturity.** You stopped over-functioning in relationships that should have been mutual from the start. You stopped being the invisible engine that kept everyone else moving while your own heart sat idling in the background.

You didn't become cold. You became precise. **And in a world that rewards women for bleeding quietly, precision is a revolution.**

The Accountability Experiment

Dropping the Ball (On Purpose)

Alright, here's where we stop spinning our wheels and start collecting evidence.

Because by now, you've got receipts. Emotional ones. A thousand quiet instances of holding it all together. You know what's happening. You feel the weight. You've named it. And now it's time to test it.

Not in a dramatic, *"I'm done doing everything!"* explosion. Not with a slammed cabinet or a passive-aggressive sigh. I'm talking about a quiet, deliberate pause. A tactical retreat. A strategic silence that gives you the one thing you haven't had in this dynamic: a clear view of what happens when *you* stop doing it all.

You let the ball drop.

Not all the balls. Just a few.

The ones he's perfectly capable of picking up if he's paying any attention.

Don't remind him about his mother's birthday card. Don't preempt the late fee on the bill that's **always** in your name because he "doesn't get how the login works." Don't top up the dog food, fix the calendar clash, or text his friend back about Saturday. Let it sit. Let it pile. Let it rot, if it must.

And say nothing.

Not in protest. Not in punishment. In curiosity.

This is **data collection**. You are not being petty; you are giving him an opportunity. You are stepping back and watching the system you've built around him, the unspoken structure that keeps your shared life moving like a well-oiled machine, and seeing what happens when you stop being the oil.

It's uncomfortable. If you're the type of woman who remembers everyone's coffee order, everyone's birthday, everyone's trauma history and dietary preference, this will feel like a betrayal. Like dropping the ball will somehow reflect poorly on **you**, not him. Like you're letting things go that you were **trained** to believe made you good, lovable, valuable.

But sis, what if that value system is the problem?

Because something's already breaking. It's been breaking in silence. Breaking in that heavy-breath moment when you realize he hasn't noticed you haven't eaten. Breaking in the part of you that's been stretching to hold it all without being asked, thanked, or even seen.

This is not a test to catch him failing.

It's a window into truth.

Does he notice the silence? Does he flinch at the tension of your absence? Does he finally stop mistaking your emotional labor for the natural rhythm of life?

Or does he do what he's always done and wait for you to reset?

What happens when the house doesn't run on autopilot?

When you stop folding his socks the "right" way?

When you stop making his stress your full-time job?

He might rise. He might stumble and course-correct. He might come to you with real ownership instead of panic, and finally say, *"I had no idea you were carrying this much. Let me help."*

And if he does? Beautiful. That's something to build on.

But if he doesn't?

If he doesn't even notice what's missing, or worse — if he notices and waits you out because that's what always worked before?

You'll know.

That's when you drop the *"Oops, I forgot too!"* turd with a smile of an angel.

The "I'm Not Doing It Anymore" Conversation

So, you dropped the ball. You didn't throw it across the room, you didn't light it on fire, you just set it down gently and walked away to see what would happen.

And surprise, surprise: **he either stepped up, stared at it like it was a foreign object, or stepped over it entirely like it was your job to clean it up anyway.**

Now you're standing in the space between silence and speech. That strange middle ground where you've already said so much with your absence, but now the moment calls for something more official. Something audible. Something undeniable.

This is where you stop carrying the emotional load **and** stop pretending it doesn't hurt.

This is where you stop whispering your needs into pillows and start naming them out loud, unapologetically.

All you need to do is to say the words that most women don't say until they're already halfway out the door:

"I'm not doing this anymore."

That's it.

No monologue. No bullet points. No PowerPoint presentation explaining the history of his emotional absenteeism.

Just one clear, powerful statement from a woman who has finally remembered her worth.

Because if you've gotten to this point, it's not because he forgot to vacuum last Tuesday. It's because you've been running a whole unacknowledged operations center behind the scenes of your relationship, and you're exhausted.

Emotionally. Mentally. Physically. Soul-deep tired.

So, when you say, *"I'm not doing this anymore,"* you're not threatening him. You're not weaponizing your love. You're not punishing anyone.

You are choosing survival. Sanity. Self-respect.

How to Say It (Without Backpedaling Like a Guilt-Ridden Gymnast)

You don't owe him a grand opening speech. But if you're someone who feels better having a script, or at least a backbone stiffener, here's one to keep in your pocket:

"I've been carrying most of the emotional and mental load in this relationship. I know it wasn't always visible, and maybe I didn't speak up before, but I'm speaking up now. I'm tired. I'm overwhelmed. And I can't keep doing everything. So I'm not. If something matters to you, you'll handle it. If it doesn't, it won't get done. But I'm done holding all of it by default."

Simple. Unapologetic. No softness required.

You're not inviting negotiation, you're delivering notification.

Don't pad it with a dozen *"I feel"* statements or sugarcoat it to protect his fragile ego. You've done enough protecting. You've buffered him from reality for long enough. Now it's his turn to feel the gravity of what it means when the woman who did it all… stops.

Here are four shifts that change everything:

From Softening to Stating

Instead of: *"I know this probably sounds silly, but…"*

Try: ***"This matters to me, and I want to talk about it."***

You're not silly. You're not fragile. You're not dramatic for having feelings. The moment you frame your needs like they might be ridiculous, you hand him permission to treat them that way. Say what's real. Own it like it's valid, because it is.

From Explaining to Naming

Instead of: *"I've just been really tired and stressed, and maybe that's why I snapped, and I know you didn't mean to..."*

Try: ***"When you dismissed what I said, I felt disrespected. That's been happening a lot, and it's wearing me down."***

Stop padding every truth with a disclaimer. You're not a liability lawyer. You're a woman telling someone how their behavior is affecting you. Be clear. Be brief. Then shut up and let the discomfort land where it needs to.

From Hinting to Holding a Standard

Instead of: *"It would be really great if you could help more... when you have time..."*

Try: ***"I can't keep doing everything. This needs to be more balanced."***

Vague suggestions are the love language of women who've been taught not to be "too much." But here's the thing — if you can't say what you actually need, don't be surprised when he doesn't deliver. This is not the time to be poetic. This is the time to be specific.

From Managing His Reaction to Trusting Your Intention

You've spent years pre-buffering every sentence, rehearsing every tone, prepping for blowback like it's a damn hostage negotiation. But what if you let the discomfort happen?

What if you stopped babysitting his reaction and just trusted that your calm, clear truth is enough?

Try this: ***"I'm not saying this to fight. I'm saying it because I care about this relationship, and I need to know you do too. I can't carry this alone anymore."***

And if he starts huffing, sulking, or twisting it into some "you're attacking me" moment?

You pause.

And say: **"This is exactly why I don't bring things up."**

Then let the silence hang.

Not because you're being cold, but because the conversation already happened. You said your piece. It's his move now.

Expect Pushback. And Hold the Damn Line.

Will he react well? Maybe.

But chances are, if your relationship has been a one-woman show, he won't.

He might look at you like you just punched a puppy. He might sulk. He might accuse you of starting drama or "changing." He might throw out the old greatest hits: *"Why are you being so distant?" "You're not the same anymore." "Is this about the dishwasher again?"*

Do. Not. Fall. For. It.

The moment you say, *"I'm not doing this anymore… unless you're mad,"* you're back in the damn loop.

Don't soften it. Don't rephrase it mid-sentence. Don't dial it down just because he makes a sad face or storms out to sit in the car.

You didn't get here by being dramatic.

You got here by being **quiet for too long**.

And now that you've found your voice, don't hand it back to him because he can't handle the volume.

If he listens? If he responds with curiosity, humility, actual change? **Amazing**. That's a relationship worth growing.

But if he tries to guilt you, gaslight you, or emotionally collapse in your lap so you're forced to soothe **him** while advocating for your own emotional survival?

Step back.

That is not partnership. That is performance. And you're not buying tickets anymore.

This moment isn't about whether he **likes** what you're saying.

It's about whether he **respects** it.

Whether he recognizes the woman in front of him isn't threatening to leave — she's daring to stay, but on **entirely different terms**.

So, say it. Say it again if you need to.

"I'm not doing this anymore."

And then?

Mean it.

Even if your voice shakes. Even if you feel like you're going to puke. Even if a piece of you still hopes he'll finally become the man you've been waiting for.

Because this isn't just a boundary.

This is the foundation of what comes next, whether that's healing the relationship or healing yourself without it.

Either way, **you win.**

CHAPTER 6:

DATA COLLECTION: TEST, DON'T CODDLE

The Data Collection Phase

Drop the Clipboard. Let Things Run Without You and See What Falls Apart

You've been the project manager of this relationship for so long, you don't even realize you're holding the clipboard anymore. It's just... there. Constantly. In your mental hand. Tracking the appointments, the groceries, the mood shifts, the family logistics, the birthdays, the dentist follow-ups, the subtle cues he always seems to miss but you never do. If you had a dollar for every behind-the-scenes task you've handled without praise, without prompting, without him even realizing it needed to be done, you'd have enough cash to hire a full-time assistant and finally disappear into that damn spa weekend you keep saying you'll book "when things calm down."

But let's not pretend the clipboard is romantic. It's not some cute love language of organization. It's not a personality quirk or a "type A" badge you wear with pride. **It's survival gear.** You've been using it to keep things functional in a system that would fall apart if you ever stopped overfunctioning. You've used it to hide the fact that this relationship only runs smoothly because you're constantly smoothing. Constantly managing. Constantly adjusting yourself around someone else's underperformance.

And you are exhausted. Not just end-of-the-week, I-need-a-nap exhausted. The kind of tired that lives in your bones. The kind that makes you stare at a wall for ten minutes because even thinking feels like effort. The kind of tired that can only be cured by finally putting down the weight you were never meant to carry alone.

So, here's what comes next: **drop the clipboard.**

Let go of the scheduling, the prompting, the gentle nudging disguised as *"babe, don't forget."* Let go of being the human Google Calendar, the invisible safety net, the one-person operations team. Stop managing the relationship like it's your full-time job with no pay and no boundaries.

And then. Just watch.

This isn't about setting traps or creating some silent protest where you secretly hope he fails just to prove a point. That's not the energy. This is about visibility. About making the invisible labor visible, not to him, but to **you**.

And yes, things might fall apart. The trash might overflow, the bills might sit unopened, the social calendar might go eerily quiet.

And as a consequence, the emotional tone of the relationship might get heavier, edgier, more uncertain.

But that's not chaos, **that's clarity.** That's the real state of things, unfiltered by your effort.

And while he might feel mildly inconvenienced or confused by the shift, you will feel something deeper. You will start to notice just how many moving parts you've been tracking, how many responsibilities you've quietly absorbed, how many moments you've been holding that were never acknowledged, because you never allowed them to be seen.

And once you've seen it all clearly, **without the blur of love, hope, or habit**, you will find yourself standing in front of the most honest question you've asked in a long time: *Do I want to keep doing this?*

Not in a bitter way. Not in a collapse. But in full awareness.

- *Do I want to keep being the only one who knows what needs to happen?*

- *Do I want to keep holding everything together while he floats along, occasionally offering praise but never sharing the load?*

- *Do I want to keep this system running, knowing it only works because I never let it stop?*

- *Or am I finally, truly ready to let some plates drop and see if he knows how to catch?*

Because **whatever breaks when you stop holding it was never balanced to begin with.**

And maybe what you need isn't to keep holding harder.

Maybe what you need is to step back, breathe deep, and let the damn clipboard hit the floor.

Silence Is Data

You're going quiet because silence… **real, uninterrupted, unnarrated silence**… is sometimes the only thing that can show you what the connection is actually made of.

What if the quiet is met with contentment, if your absence of effort is simply absorbed as comfort, if he mistakes your silence for peace instead of absence?

That's your answer.

He's been allowed to live inside a system that always worked without him needing to notice how or why. A system you designed, maintained, and quietly resented until now.

Silence is not withdrawal. It's data. It's truth. It's what lives underneath the scripts and speeches and carefully curated moments of emotional caretaking.

Let it stretch. Let it echo. Let it breathe.

And this time?

Don't interrupt it just because he's uncomfortable. Don't rush to fill the space just because you're used to being the one who makes everything feel okay. Let it speak. Let it linger. Let it show you what's real.

Don't fix, don't guide, don't coach. Just observe.

If emotional coaching were a billable service, you'd have a waitlist three months long, a passive income stream, and a top-ranked podcast by now.

You don't need to spell out, again, how the gap between his words and actions is starting to eat you alive.

He knows. You know he knows.

He's not confused. He's not unaware. He's simply never had to **show** that awareness because you've always stepped in with the flashcards and the scripts and the gentle nudge that says, *"Here, try this instead."*

Now you stop.

You don't prompt, don't walk him through it, don't translate your pain into more palatable language, don't shrink your frustration into a tone that feels less threatening. And you don't jump in when he hesitates, or soften the silence when he avoids the hard thing.

Instead, you sit still. And you observe.

This is your data collection phase.

- Does he take initiative without being nudged?

- Does he manage his own emotional landscape without your forecast and first-aid kit?

- Does he engage like a partner, or wait for your signal?

And yes, it's uncomfortable. Deeply, viscerally uncomfortable. Especially when you've built your identity around competence, around knowing how to fix things, around being the one who always sees it coming and steps in before it crashes. But **this is the part you can't skip**. Because if you're always stepping in to correct, or clarify, or motivate, you'll never really know what he's capable of or what he's unwilling to do unless someone else makes it easy.

And that's the core question now.

Not *"Can I help him get there?"* But ***"Is he willing to get there on his own?"***

Does he step forward? Does he falter and course-correct?

Does he stand still, waiting for you to resume your usual role?

Whatever it is, **you'll see it**.

And when you finally let go of managing his growth and just watch, not with judgment, but with clarity, you'll stop asking questions you already knew the answers to.

Because once you see the truth without all your effort shaping it?

You'll be done guessing. And maybe, just maybe, done fixing, too.

Mirror His Energy Without the Drama

Match His Forgetfulness with Your Own — "Oops, I Forgot Too"

You ever notice how his *'Sorry, I forgot'* gets treated like a harmless quirk — almost endearing — while yours becomes a referendum on your capability?

Curious how that works.

Maybe it's time for a little mirroring exercise. Not to get even, not to spark chaos or play games. Just to reflect, with complete emotional neutrality, the rhythm you've both settled into, **one where remembering is optional for him because you've made it mandatory for yourself.**

So now? You forget too.

You forget to send the birthday message to his cousin. You forget to follow up on that dinner plan. You forget to build your life around his ever-shifting moods and loosely promised plans.

You stop mentally clocking all the invisible tasks you usually pre-emptively solve. You stop padding the schedule, filling in the blanks, catching the curveballs before they land.

"Oops, I forgot too."

With a calm, level tone that says: this is the energy we're working with now. This is the balance you've shown me. This is me stepping out of an unpaid role I was never meant to hold and seeing what happens when I give exactly what I get.

Because this isn't sabotage. **It's symmetry.**

It's allowing the ripple effects of your non-effort to echo in the same way his have echoed into your stress, your mental load, your sense that if you ever dropped the ball, the whole game would fall apart. And if he suddenly panics, if he realizes the thing didn't get done, the plan didn't fall into place, the moment didn't get remembered, it's not your job to step in with an apology or a fix.

It's your cue to say, calmly, *"Oh, I used to handle that. I figured you had it."*

And then let it sit. Let the awkwardness bloom. Let the silence stretch into something revealing. Because in that silence, what becomes clear isn't just the missed task — it's the imbalance. It's the gap. It's the space where your labor used to be, and how empty things feel without it.

If he's allowed to forget without consequence, then so are you.

If he calls it neglect when you stop showing up with the same unthanked effort you've always given, then what he's reacting to isn't the task. **It's the loss of your overfunctioning. It's the discomfort of realizing how much of the relationship has been riding on you.** And if he can't handle that, if your quiet neutrality feels threatening instead of fair, then that isn't a reflection of your forgetfulness.

That's a reflection of his entitlement.

So let the silence speak, let the system glitch, let the gap show up where your effort used to be.

And if he finally sees the missing pieces, if he finally notices the water's gone still and starts to ask why, then maybe, just maybe, he'll remember what's been slipping through the cracks this entire time:

You.

Read the Results Like a Grown-Ass Woman

Watch What Changes, And What Doesn't, Without You in the Driver's Seat

This is the part no one prepares you for… not the silence that happens on the outside, but the kind that starts **inside your chest** when you finally stop steering, stop nudging, stop trying to predict and prevent and perfect the entire relationship by sheer will and love and exhaustion. It's not just that you've gone quiet, it's that your entire nervous system has stepped off duty, and for the first time in a long time, you're not secretly scripting how the next scene is supposed to go.

You're not reacting, not rescuing, not filling in the blanks before he notices they were even there. You're not smoothing the edge of his stress with careful tone shifts. You're not compensating for his disconnection by over-connecting on both sides. You're not preloading the apology you think he might need, or managing the vibe in advance so he doesn't shut down again.

You've stepped all the way out of the driver's seat.

And it is uncomfortable as hell, because your reflex is to lean forward, to grab the wheel, to make sure this thing doesn't swerve into a wall, but now you're sitting back, arms crossed, watching the wheel wobble, the speed change, where the momentum goes when **you're not the one supplying it.**

This is where **you start seeing what's real.**

You see whether he picks up the things you quietly set down.

You see whether he notices the shift in rhythm, not just because you stopped talking, but because he actually **feels something is missing —**

your presence, your labor, your energy that's no longer pouring into making everything seamless.

And if he doesn't?

If the tasks go untouched, if the air stays stale, if the silence just becomes more comfortable for him now that you're no longer "on his back," if the ease of you doing less simply becomes his cue to do even less too, then that's your answer.

And that's the data you never had when you were too busy spinning all the plates, because when you're the one generating the motion, it's impossible to know what happens when you stop.

And if something shifts — not in performance, not in panic, not in an *"I'll change"* meltdown, but in the small, consistent actions that tell you **he gets it now**, that he's not waiting to be coached or caught or reminded, then maybe you've got something to rebuild.

Not a fantasy, not a fairy tale, but a **possibility**.

A baseline that no longer depends on you doing 90% of the emotional labor just to keep things upright.

That's what this moment was always about — to see.

To see what happens when you stop adjusting the entire system to protect his comfort and finally let the imbalance become visible. And when the scaffolding of your over-functioning falls away, when the props collapse, when the energy stops flowing from only one side—you get to find out if there's a foundation, or just an empty shell where you once imagined a future.

You've been the driver for too long.

Now sit down. Fold your hands in your lap.

And watch who grabs the wheel. And if no one reaches for it? If no one steps up, adjusts course, or even notices that the ride feels different now?

Then at least now you know. And knowing will always be kinder than guessing.

Red Flags vs. Repairable Dynamics: How to Tell the Difference

This will seem weird… but there's a place in relationships that no one warns you about — a soul-sucking little purgatory between "not bad enough to leave" and "not good enough to feel okay."

Where you're not in a screaming match every night, but you also can't remember the last time you felt safe exhaling next to him.

Where nothing is technically *wrong*, but something is *definitely* not right.

You find yourself in that gray zone, second-guessing everything — your standards, your memories, your gut.

You tell yourself, *"He's not abusive." "He's not cheating." "He means well."*

And then, of course, my favorite one: ***"Maybe I'm overreacting."***

Babe. You're not.

You're just stuck in the confusion trap — a silent war between your nervous system and your logic. One half of you is screaming, ***"This isn't sustainable,"*** while the other half is whispering, ***"But he's trying…"***

So, let's make it simple. Let's separate what's survivable from what's sacred. Let's draw a goddamn line between red flags and repairable dynamics, because one means you're in danger of losing yourself. The other means there's still something real to work with.

A red flag isn't just a flaw, it's a pattern that erodes you.

It's not one bad day. It's not one snarky comment. It's not forgetting your birthday or messing up dinner plans.

It's the **repeated, unchanging** behaviors that slowly, silently make you question your sanity. It's when you start to wonder if you're the difficult one because you've been emotionally contorting yourself into a human pretzel just to keep the peace.

Red flags are sneaky like that. They wear normal clothes.

They say the right things. But they leave you hollow.

Red flags sound like this in your head:

- *"I can't bring that up, he'll twist it into being my fault."*

- *"If I say how I feel, he'll withdraw, and I'll have to fix it."*

- *"Why do I feel lonelier next to him than I do alone?"*

And they look like this in practice:

- You're constantly rehearsing your tone before hard conversations.

- He punishes vulnerability with distance or mood swings.

- You start doubting your own reactions, even when something hurt.

- He keeps flipping the blame, like your pain is an inconvenience instead of information.

- You feel like you're auditioning for your own relationship, over and over again.

And here's the wild part: even when things are calm, it still feels off. Because red flags don't always shout. Sometimes they whisper: *"Shrink. Adjust. Don't stir the water."*

Repairable Dynamics Come With Accountability, Not Apologies (aka Green Flags)

Imperfections? Totally normal. Missteps? Of course.

Even good men can mess up. But the difference… the **real**, felt difference… is in how they handle it.

When something is repairable, the effort feels steady. Not performative. Not reactive. Not convenient.

You'll know it's repairable when:

- He listens to **understand**, not to defend.

- He **brings things up later**, showing he didn't just hear you, he actually thought about it.

- He changes the behavior, not just the mood.

- He doesn't need a crisis to do the bare minimum.

- Your truth doesn't threaten him, it invites him to rise.

In repairable relationships, you feel **less** afraid to speak up over time, not more.

You start to breathe easier, not hold your breath. You still have conflicts, sure, but the aftermath isn't worse than the argument.

There's repair. There's reflection. There's **movement.**

You're still yourself in the relationship. Not a ghost version. Not a shell.

But What If He's "Trying"?

Let's talk about this one for a second.

Because a lot of women stay way too long in relationships that are slowly killing them emotionally, all because of **potential.** Because he **cried** once when you said you were tired. Because he **said** he wants to be better.

Because he **meant it**, right?

But here's the thing — "trying" doesn't count if it only happens when you're halfway out the door. It doesn't count if it lasts three days and then vanishes into thin air. It doesn't count if it's all talk, no traction.

Real trying looks like:

- Boring consistency

- Accountability without theatrics

- Quiet adjustments that don't need to be praised

- Showing up when there's **no threat of losing you**

Trying isn't a one-man performance. It's a long-ass series of small shifts that don't rely on your exhaustion to be activated.

So, if you're feeling more **guilty** than **seen**, more like a coach than a partner, more like you're monitoring progress than enjoying connection — you're not in a repair loop.

You're in a guilt spiral. And it will keep you stuck for years.

The Six-Month Test

Still unsure? Ask yourself this:

If nothing changes... if this is what the relationship stays like for the next six months, would I stay?

Don't ask:

- *"Does he love me?"*

- *"Does he have potential?"*

- *"Is this just a rough patch?"*

Ask: ***"Do I feel safe, seen, and supported as I am, today?"***

If the answer is no, then it's a **red flag**. Even if he doesn't mean harm. Even if he's sweet in other ways. Even if you love him to the bone.

And if the answer is yes, and you're both genuinely showing up, doing the work, owning your shit, and building something real? Then maybe… **maybe**… you've got a foundation worth standing on.

But don't you dare build that foundation on your own back.

Don't you dare keep justifying emotional starvation because he **meant** to feed you but forgot to bring a spoon.

And once you can tell a red flag from a repairable crack, you stop patching bullet holes with optimism.

That's where Part II ends, with a deep breath and a decision to reclaim every bit of power you gave away in the name of hope.

And what comes next?

That's where we go in Part III.

Because now that you've paused the cycle and seen the truth behind the emotional scaffolding, it's time to step back into your own story—not as the background character in someone else's healing arc, but as the main event in your own.

Let's rebuild.

A Tiny Favor That Helps the Next Woman (and Future You)

If one chapter so far made you exhale, laugh, or whisper "holy hell, that's me," you just found something most people never get — clarity.

Would you help the next reader find hers faster?

Your one-minute review helps, for real:

- One more woman realizes overfunctioning isn't love.

- One more heart chooses peace instead of panic.

- One more person finally stops mistaking anxiety for chemistry.

- One more reader feels a little less alone.

Amazon doesn't care how loud I shout. It listens to you.

Your words are the map that leads someone else here when she needs it most.

What to Write (keep it human)

- One sentence about what hit home.

- One tool or truth you're actually using.

- Who you'd tell to read this next.

That's it. No essays. No overthinking.

Sixty seconds of your time = one woman's turning point.

Ready?

Point your camera at the QR code ↓

Thank you for paying it forward.

You didn't just review a book—you handed someone her clarity a few chapters early.

Want to Stay in Touch?

I only write when I have a new book coming out — no fluff, no spam, no performative "you got this" emails. Hand on heart!

Join the list here ↓

You'll be the first to know when the next book is out… and maybe, just maybe, it'll find you right when you need it.

PART III:

THE BREAKUP WITH THE ROLE, NOT JUST THE RELATIONSHIP

CHAPTER 7:

PUT DOWN THE BACKPACK, SIS

The Strong Woman Lie

You've been carrying both of you. Now it's time to carry yourself.

So, you did it.

You dropped the damn ball. You stepped back. You stopped micromanaging his manhood and let the silence speak louder than your most well-worded texts ever could. You pulled back—not to punish him, but to give him space to step forward. You made room. You made room again. You waited. You hoped. You watched.

And he did… nothing.

Or maybe he did something, but not nearly enough. Not enough to rebuild trust. Not enough to lighten your load. Not enough to make you feel like an actual **partner** instead of his emotional side hustle. And now you're here, staring at the same mess, except this time you're no longer willing to clean it up. Not because you're cold. But because you're finally clear.

You wanted to stay. You really did. You loved him. You **wanted** this to work. But love without effort is just a slow form of self-abandonment, and you've already done enough of that.

This isn't the part where you become bitter. This is the part where you become **done**.

This is the quiet, exhausted, heartbreakingly adult decision to stop dragging a relationship up a hill that was never meant to be yours to climb alone. This is where you stop performing "strength" like it's some badge of honor and start realizing that the strongest thing you'll ever do is **walk away from the job you never applied for**.

So, if you're reading this wondering, *"How do I let go when I've poured so much in?"*

The answer is simple, and also brutal:

You put down the backpack.

And then you take one step forward.

Even if your knees shake.

Even if your heart breaks.

Even if a small part of you still whispers, **maybe he'll change**.

Because this chapter?

This is where you stop waiting for him to show up…

…and finally show up for **yourself**.

You were told being needed meant being loved.

This is where we talk about the scam of the century: being "the strong one."

You didn't apply for this title. No one sat you down and asked if you were interested in being the one who holds shit together while everyone else falls apart. But somehow, somewhere between being praised for your maturity and applauded for your resilience, you got handed the crown — and the chains that came with it.

And at first? You wore it proudly. You thought, *"Hell yeah, I'm strong."* You were proud that you could juggle work, relationships, bills, kids, drama, emotional damage, and still show up with clean hair and some kind of meal on the table, even if it was just toast and wine. You got things done. You showed up when no one else did. You remembered the appointments, sent the birthday texts, fixed the vibe in the room, and carried the emotional load like it was just part of being a decent human.

People leaned on you. Partners depended on you. Friends called you a "rock" like that was supposed to be a compliment and not a warning sign. You got so used to hearing, "I don't know what I'd do without you," that you started thinking it meant love. Spoiler: it meant dependence. Not the same thing.

But here's the quiet, nasty truth: **the stronger you appeared, the less support you received.**

The more you handled, the less anyone even thought to ask if you were okay.

Because you didn't look like someone who needed help. You looked like someone who had it all together. You were the one people vented to. The one who "never breaks." The one who gets left to pick up the pieces **because you always have.**

And let me tell you something brutal: **strength, when unacknowledged and unreciprocated, will bury you.**

Because underneath all that praise and admiration is a woman who is fucking tired. Not just "long week at work" tired. Existential, bone-deep, can't-remember-what-it's-like-to-be-held tired.

And the worst part? You can't even complain.

Because the moment you do, if you so much as say *"I'm overwhelmed"*, people look at you like you've grown a second head. *"But you're so strong!"* they say, like that's some kind of antidote to burnout. Like your ability to withstand bullshit is the same thing as wanting to live in it.

And here's a truth bomb for you: **the strong woman archetype is a trap.** It convinces you that your worth is measured in how much you can carry, how much you can endure, how quietly you can suffer without becoming "too much."

You start thinking asking for help is weakness. That setting boundaries is selfish. That needing anything — rest, space, emotional safety — makes you a burden.

Strong women don't get to fall apart. They don't get softness or rescue. They get a gold star for surviving shit they never should've had to survive in the first place.

So, here's your permission slip: **you can put the damn crown down.**

You don't have to be the strong one anymore. Not in this relationship. Not in this chapter. Not for people who benefit from your silence and then call it grace.

You can say, *"I'm tired."*

You can say, *"I need help."*

You can say, *"I'm not doing this anymore."*

You can cry without apologizing for the tears. You can walk away from the person who only loved you for what you could do for them. You can stop proving your strength through self-abandonment.

Because the truth is? You were never weak for needing rest. Or selfish for wanting support, or dramatic for saying *"this is too much."*

You were just told that being strong meant being silent.

And that, my dear, was the biggest f*cking lie of all.

Burnout Isn't a Badge of Honor

There's this twisted little myth that somehow snuck into the bloodstream of womanhood, quietly passed down like a family heirloom: the idea that **exhaustion means you're doing it right.**

Like if you're not crawling into bed at night feeling like your soul just got wrung out like a dishcloth, you didn't give enough. Like running on fumes is some kind of moral high ground. Like being emotionally, mentally, and physically tapped out is what "good women" do.

Girl… NO. Just… no.

Burnout is not noble. It's not proof of love. It's not a sign that you're loyal, dedicated, or worthy. It's a sign that **you've been living in a system that has no intention of giving back what you keep pouring in.**

And if your relationship only works when you're over-functioning, over-giving, and over-explaining while your partner coasts in the glow of your unpaid labor, then that's not a partnership. That's a hostage situation with better lighting.

The worst part? Society applauds you for it.

They love a woman who "does it all." They'll call you inspiring while you quietly fall apart, repost memes about self-care but still expect you to carry the mental load of five people and look hot doing it, or tell you, *"You're so strong,"* when what they really mean is, *"It's convenient that you don't complain."*

And somewhere along the way, you start to believe it. You start to believe that rest is indulgent. That needing help is weakness. That if you stop moving, even for a second, everything will collapse, because, spoiler alert, it probably will. You've been holding it all up.

But here's the thing: **if your rest equals collapse, that means you weren't in a relationship. You were in a one-woman show with a spectator who clapped at intermission.**

And baby, applause doesn't refill your tank.

You don't get medals for burnout. You don't get love points for how much bullshit you quietly tolerate. You don't win anything for being the woman who never drops the ball, except maybe a lifetime of resentment and a stress-induced ulcer.

You don't have to earn rest by being on the brink of a breakdown.

You don't have to reach full-blown collapse to be allowed to take a breath. You don't have to prove you've suffered enough to justify stepping back.

Rest is not a reward. It's a right.

You are not a machine that gets recharged just enough to keep going until the next meltdown. You're a human being. One with limits. One with needs. One with the right to stop **before** you hit the wall.

And the next time someone wants to crown you the queen of doing too much, feel free to hand that crown back and say: ***"I'm done collecting badges for bleeding out. I want peace. Not applause."***

You Don't Have to Earn Rest

Somewhere along the line, you were taught — maybe not in words, but definitely in tone, in glances, in who got praised and who got quietly judged — that rest is something you only get after you've bled yourself dry for everyone else. After the workday. After the vacuuming. After the kids are asleep. After you've picked up the emotional slack for the third week in a row and still remembered to text his mum for her birthday. You were trained to treat rest like a prize at the bottom of a cereal box: cheap, small, and only available once you've dug through all the crap.

But rest is not a reward.

And you? You are not a robot with a checklist taped to her spine, only allowed to sit down when the green light blinks.

You are a human being. One with a nervous system. One with a body that whispers and aches and sometimes screams. One with a spirit that's sick of being background noise to everyone else's main character energy.

And still, the second you pause — just for a breath, a scroll, a stretch, a full-on lie-down with one hand flung dramatically across your face like a Victorian ghost — the guilt shows up like it pays rent. Loud. Righteous. Annoyingly familiar.

It reminds you of what you didn't do yet. Of what someone might think. Of how he's been sulking for two days and now **you** look like the one who doesn't care. It's the voice that tells you rest is something to be earned through perfect behavior and sacrificial exhaustion. That you don't get to rest until everyone else is happy, stable, fed, nurtured, and fully satisfied. Which, newsflash, means never.

So, this is your rebellion. This is your quiet, tired, slightly defiant refusal to keep proving your value through depletion. This is where you stop performing resilience and start honoring reality. That you're tired. That you're allowed to be tired. That you don't have to collapse in public or cry in the laundry room or forget a birthday or get sick to justify taking a f*cking break.

And no, it won't look pretty. You might still have dishes in the sink. You might still have unanswered emails. You might still be mid-fight with a partner who thinks silence is strategy and conflict resolution is **your job**.

But even then — especially then — you are allowed to pause. Right now. In the mess. In the middle. Before the burnout. Without permission. Without applause.

And yeah, maybe someone will be annoyed. Maybe your partner will grumble. Maybe the world won't slow down just because you finally did. But here's what matters more than all of that: nothing will burn if you rest. And if it does? It was already on fire—you just weren't watching because you were too busy putting out everyone else's.

So, rest. Even when it's awkward. Even when it feels unnatural. Even when the guilt buzzes under your skin like a swarm of "shoulds."

Because rest is not optional. It's not indulgent. It's not selfish. It's sacred. It's boundary-setting in its quietest form. It's you saying, *"I am not the emergency contact for everyone's emotional crisis anymore."* It's you saying, *"I'm allowed to be horizontal without a fever or an excuse."* It's you deciding that your worth isn't connected to your usefulness, and that exhaustion isn't a personality trait.

This isn't about becoming a minimalist monk or running away to Bali. This is about taking five damn minutes to be still without apology. Sitting down in your own life. Not to strategize or plan or regroup. **But to just be.** To breathe. To exist without performing. To let the moment be soft, even if the rest of the day isn't.

And when the world keeps spinning and nothing explodes? That's when it hits you: all this time, you were the engine. And now, finally, you get to pull over.

So, pull over.

Put the phone down. Turn the noise off. Let the guilt pass like weather. And let your body remember what it feels like to be a woman who does not have to collapse in order to justify the pause.

No justification. No checklist. No gold star.

Just rest.

Because you're done earning what was always yours.

Who Are You Without the Fixing?

Reclaim Your Identity from the "Helper" Role

You've been the helper for so long, it's not just what you do — it's who you've quietly, unconsciously become. It's woven into the way you enter a room and instantly scan for what needs doing, who's upset, what vibe needs fixing. It's in how you anticipate the blow-ups before they happen, how you fill in the blanks no one asked you to fill, how you carry the mental load like a damn supercomputer quietly running in the background while everyone else coasts.

And you've been praised for it. Rewarded for it. Treated like the MVP of emotional labor and logistical management. So much so that over time, it started to feel like a compliment when really, it was a leash.

Because they weren't seeing **you**. They were seeing your usefulness.

You weren't loved unconditionally, you were loved transactionally.

You were loved **for**. For being calm under pressure. For never needing too much. For being easy, low-maintenance, "so strong." And slowly, that became the metric. The identity. The box you kept squeezing yourself into because you learned early — maybe even before you had words for it — that love came easiest when you made other people's lives easier.

And now? **You don't know how to exist without it.** Without the role. Without the reflex to jump in, smooth it out, carry the weight, and then smile like it didn't crush you.

But here's the thing no one told you: being helpful isn't a personality. It's a survival strategy.

It's a well-honed adaptation that once protected you, maybe even saved you, but now? Now it's become a trap.

Because the more you overfunction, the more people around you underfunction. The more you show up, the less they have to. And the more you prioritize being "the strong one," the less space there is for you to be human.

So, if you're feeling empty lately… like you're doing everything **right** and still feel invisible, maybe it's because the role you've been playing is blocking the connection you actually crave.

And unlearning it? It's messy.

You'll disappoint people, confuse them. They'll wonder what happened to the easygoing version of you who never said no, never asked for too much, never made a fuss.

But let them wonder.

Let them sit in the discomfort of not being served.

Because every time you override your needs to preserve their comfort, you reinforce the idea that your worth is in what you do, not who you are.

You don't owe anyone your constant availability. You don't need to justify your "no." You don't need to fix, help, soothe, soften, or spin plates for people who would let them crash the second you walked away.

It's okay to let the ball drop.

It's okay to watch someone else stumble and *not* rush in to catch them.

It's okay to ask yourself, "Is this mine to carry?" and realize the answer is no.

Because the truth is, when you stop defining your identity by how useful you are to others, you finally create room to be useful to yourself.

To your own joy.

To your own needs.

To your own goddamn dreams that got shoved to the bottom of the list because someone else needed a ride, a favor, a therapist, or a rescue from their latest mess.

This isn't about becoming selfish.

It's about becoming whole.

It's about breaking up with the version of you that thought being needed was the same thing as being loved.

You can still be kind.

You can still care deeply.

But you get to put yourself on the list too.

So, the next time your reflex is to jump in, to overfunction, to pick up the emotional slack before anyone even notices it exists—pause.

Breathe.

And remember: you're not the helper.

You're a human being.

And you don't need to save the world just to earn a seat in it.

You're Allowed to Be Held, Not Just Be the Holder

There's a kind of tired that sleep doesn't touch — the kind that comes from always being the one others count on, always being the grounded one, the responsible one, the emotionally available one. And while that role might look strong on the outside, the inside often tells a different story — a quiet ache that builds not just from the weight you carry, but from the haunting absence of anyone willing to **carry you**.

Because when you've spent a lifetime being the one who holds everything and everyone together, you start to forget what it even feels like to be held yourself, not just physically, in a hug or a passing squeeze on the shoulder, but emotionally, deeply, in the kind of way where **someone meets your mess without flinching**, without rushing to fix it, without needing you to shrink it down to something palatable.

And maybe you've started to believe that kind of comfort isn't available to you. That the trade-off for being "the strong one" is that you don't get to fall apart. That your role is to nod and smile and say "I'm good" even when your insides are unraveling like a threadbare sweater you're scared to tug on.

It's not your fault. You didn't make this dynamic up out of nowhere. You became the emotional anchor because someone had to be. You learned early that your value was in your stability, in your ability to hold it all, in your skill at absorbing everyone else's pain without letting yours spill over. You got good at it — so good that now, when your own sadness shows up, you barely recognize it before you've already shoved it aside and picked up someone else's load instead.

But here's what no one told you while they were piling on their needs and calling you amazing: **you're not just allowed to be supported — you *need* to be.** You're not failing anyone by needing comfort. You don't have to be in crisis to justify collapsing. You don't need to offer context or caveats or excuses to be wrapped in care that doesn't come with strings attached.

It's okay to ask for softness.

It's okay to say, *"I'm not okay,"* and not immediately minimize it with a joke or a to-do list or a perfectly timed redirect.

It's okay to crave being nurtured in the same way you've shown up for everyone else.

And if that makes some people uncomfortable? If your vulnerability feels inconvenient to those who only knew you as the helper, the fixer, the one who always had her shit together, then maybe the discomfort isn't yours to carry. Maybe it belongs to the people who got too used to seeing you as a function instead of a human being.

Because this isn't about flipping the script and becoming the one who **always** needs holding. It's about recognizing that your capacity to hold others doesn't cancel out your right to be held in return. It's about re-writing the story that says love is something you have to earn through usefulness, patience, or silence.

Sometimes healing begins not with action, but with stillness.

Not with doing more, but with **allowing** more.

Allowing yourself to be a little messy. A little raw. A little broken open without needing to patch yourself up before anyone sees you bleed.

And if the person you're with can't sit with that? If they shrink when you need softness? If they only lean in when you're strong and pull back the moment you get real?

Then maybe that's your sign that you've been settling for too little.

You've held so much. You've been the calm in so many storms. You've offered steadiness to people who couldn't even name their own chaos.

It's your turn now.

Your turn to lay it down. Your turn to stop narrating strength as your default mode. Your turn to be met, to be held, to be loved not for how little you need, but for who you are when your needs finally get a seat at the table.

Let someone hold you.

And if no one will?

Then at the very least, hold space for yourself like your life depends on it.

Because it does.

Peace Might Feel Boring at First. That's Healing

Let's get one thing clear, because your brain might still be running old software while your body's trying to update, just because a relationship isn't drenched in drama, scattered with shouting matches, or soaked in that panicked, heart-thumping feeling that used to pass for connection, doesn't mean it's broken or lacking or lifeless. It might just mean… you're finally safe.

But safety, when you've spent years tethered to emotional volatility, doesn't always feel like safety. Sometimes, it feels like a glitch. It feels wrong. Flat. Empty, even. You walk into a calm, stable moment with someone who sees you, hears you, texts you back, and doesn't punish you with silence or sarcasm when they're overwhelmed, and instead of relief, you feel this low-grade discomfort buzzing under your skin like something must be missing. Something must be off.

Because when you've been surviving on high-alert for years, your nervous system becomes fluent in tension. It calibrates to chaos. It learns that love feels like confusion, urgency, emotional maintenance, and constantly earning your place. So, when the drama stops, when the adrenaline drops, and there's nothing left to fix or soothe or decode, your whole body starts whispering, **Is this it? This can't be it.**

But that whisper? That discomfort? That's not boredom. That's your body panicking in the absence of crisis. That's your brain trying to interpret peace using the language of chaos it was taught as a child, or a teenager, or a woman who once learned that love was a job with no off-switch.

Peace is unfamiliar. That's all. It's not bad. It's just **different**. It's not lacking depth. It's just not demanding blood.

And I know you've been praised for your emotional intelligence, your patience, your ability to "read the room" and make chaos feel like calm for everyone else, but now that you're sitting in real calm, the kind you didn't have to earn or orchestrate, you're realizing how exhausting all that effort actually was.

So, let's say this out loud, even if it feels strange in your mouth: **you don't need to be in crisis to be in love.** You don't need the ups and downs to feel desired. You don't have to fight to feel worthy of being chosen. That high-intensity, on-the-edge kind of love you got used to? That wasn't passion. That was survival mode with lipstick on.

And yes, healing feels awkward as hell at first. It feels like a room with no noise, no fires to put out, no emotional quicksand. It feels like sitting across from someone who's not trying to win or wound, just be with you. It feels like long silences that don't carry sharp edges. Like boring Saturday mornings that don't implode by 3 PM. Like slow affection that isn't earned with self-abandonment.

It feels like your body finally having time to unclench, and not knowing what to do with itself.

You might still find yourself wanting to poke at the peace, to test it, to stir up a little friction just to feel something, anything, because that's how your nervous system learned to recognize "aliveness." But if you can sit through that twitchy restlessness, if you can breathe through the discomfort of not having to fix or fight or earn, something starts to shift. You start to realize that this quiet isn't emptiness. It's healing. It's your new baseline.

Eventually, you stop holding your breath waiting for the next emotional ambush.

Eventually, you stop interpreting stability as dullness.

Eventually, your nervous system starts to recalibrate... slowly, gently, miraculously — to calm.

And when it does, when your body finally stops flinching at kindness, when your mind stops expecting sabotage in the silence, you'll understand what was really happening this whole time: it wasn't that peace was boring. It was that your trauma couldn't recognize safety yet.

But now it can.

And now? You get to call that safety home.

What Safe Feels Like (And How to Tell if It's Possible)

Peace and Boredom Are Not the Same Thing

There's this quiet moment… usually in the aftermath of some emotional hurricane you didn't realize you were living in until the wind finally stops… where you catch yourself sitting in silence, not tensed up, not scanning for landmines, not rehearsing your next sentence three times in your head to avoid setting something off… **just still**.

And somehow, it feels suspicious.

Because nothing's wrong. And your body? It doesn't believe it.

You're not in trouble. You're not about to be ambushed by a mood swing or a passive-aggressive sigh or a 45-minute silence treatment that starts because you asked a question with the "wrong" tone. You're just… here. Safe.

And for women like us, the ones who've trained ourselves to read between lines that were never written, to forecast storms before they've even formed, to hold space for two emotional systems while minimizing our own, it feels off. Not because something bad is happening, but because **nothing** is.

And that nothing? It can feel like boredom at first. It can feel like numbness. Like the air went too still, and you forgot how to breathe without bracing.

But hear me loud and clear:

Peace isn't boring. Your nervous system is just detoxing from dysfunction.

You've been so conditioned to equate adrenaline with love, and anxiety with aliveness, that when your heart stops racing, you worry it must be dying. When the chaos goes quiet, you assume it's just gearing up for the next explosion. When the peace arrives, you don't trust it—because you've only ever known love through the lens of "survive this moment and call it connection."

But that thing you've been calling "passion"? That wasn't passion. That was cortisol in a cute outfit. That was your fight-or-flight response wrapped in romantic tension.

Peace doesn't feel like boredom. Peace feels like not flinching.

Backed by Science

When you've lived in fight-or-flight, calm feels foreign. The brain's reward circuits confuse **predictable peace** with boredom because adrenaline withdrawal mimics emptiness.

As your nervous system recalibrates, stillness stops feeling like danger, it starts feeling like home.

It feels like:

- Hearing his keys in the door and not holding your breath.

- Saying what's on your mind without rehearsing it 12 times in your head.

- Knowing that a disagreement won't leave you sleeping with one eye open.

- Feeling your body *relax* when he walks into the room, not tighten.

- Letting silence be silence — not punishment or tension, just quiet.

But if you've never had that before? If your love life has been a nonstop episode of "emotional project management meets hostage negotiation"? Then calm will absolutely feel like something's missing. And what's missing is the constant pressure to perform. The dance. The decoding. The unspoken job of keeping the temperature just right so he doesn't blow a fuse.

It's weird to sit in a moment where everything's fine and **not be on edge**. This is when safe feels unsafe. You start second-guessing it. You poke at the calm like a bruise, wondering if it's real. You might even stir shit up just to feel **something**, because the emptiness of peace feels scarier than the chaos you've always known how to survive.

That doesn't mean you're broken. It means you're healing.

It means you're learning what it feels like to stop managing someone else's emotional weather and just… exist. Breathe. Speak. Be.

It means that maybe — just maybe — you've found something steady enough that your nervous system hasn't caught up yet.

And when you do catch up? When your body starts trusting that safety is real?

You'll stop confusing neutrality for a red flag.

You'll stop chasing chaos because you think love has to be dramatic to be deep.

You'll stop mistaking adrenaline for chemistry, and finally understand what it feels like to be loved without needing to prove you're worthy of it every five minutes.

So, if it feels boring at first? Good. That means you're not flinching.

That means you're not shrinking.

That means peace is knocking… and you're finally in a place quiet enough to hear it.

Letting Go Is a Love Language (For Yourself)

Release Isn't Revenge, It's Self-Respect

We love to pretend that walking away is this cinematic, empowered, badass move, like you're supposed to strut out the door with your lipstick perfect and your playlist queued, leaving a stunned man in your dust, full of regret and yearning, as the camera pans out on your glow-up. But in real life, walking away doesn't feel like a highlight reel. **It feels like grief.** It feels like second-guessing your own sanity. It feels like waking up at 3 a.m. with your heart racing, retracing every step that led you here, wondering if maybe, just maybe… you were too harsh, too emotional, too fast, too much.

It feels like guilt. Like loss. Like the quiet kind of devastation that doesn't even have the decency to come with a clear bad guy.

Because the truth is, you didn't want to leave. You didn't want to be the one who gave up. You wanted this to work. You were willing to do the hard parts, the messy parts, the deeply unglamorous emotional labor of growing with someone. But what you eventually had to admit, after one too many apologies with no follow-through, after one too many moments where your pain was invisible and your needs felt like burdens, is that you were growing alone.

And somewhere in that slow-burn heartbreak, you realized something that changed everything: you weren't walking away to hurt him. **You were walking away because staying was hurting *you.***

Letting go wasn't about revenge or making a point or getting some kind of karmic satisfaction out of watching him spiral without you. It was about honoring the part of you that had been quietly screaming for relief while you kept telling yourself to hang in a little longer, to be a little more understanding, to give just one more chance. It was about finally choosing your own peace over the chaos you had normalized. It was about saying, *"I'm done,"* and actually meaning it because you started loving yourself more.

There were moments when it felt like failure, because women are conditioned to see endurance as virtue, to treat their tolerance as proof of their loyalty, to believe that if a relationship ends, they must have broken it. But walking away from something that was already bleeding out doesn't make you a villain. It makes you conscious.

So, if he wants to interpret your exit as cruelty, let him. If he chooses to focus on your silence instead of the thousand things you said that were ignored, let him. If he tells himself you left out of anger, out of spite, out of some manipulative test — fine. That story's not yours to correct. Because you know the truth: you left out of clarity. You left out of self-preservation. You left because you finally understood that saving him wasn't saving you.

And if your absence burns more than your presence ever did, it's the emotional gap revealing itself now that you're no longer filling it. That ache he feels? That weight? That's not something you caused. That's something you **used to carry**.

You don't need to slam the door. You don't need a closing statement or a mic-drop moment. Your leaving is the closure. Your peace is the punctuation. You get to step away not as some stoic martyr or vengeful heroine, but as a woman who's simply done bleeding for someone who never learned to stop cutting.

Release is not a performance. It's not a scheme. It's not a threat.

It's a quiet, defiant act of self-respect.

And you didn't walk away because he deserved to lose you.

You walked away because you finally understood you didn't deserve to lose yourself.

Sometimes the Healthiest Thing You Can Do… Is Nothing

Let's just strip away the shame from this right now — doing nothing doesn't mean you're weak, or checked out, or emotionally immature. It doesn't mean you've given up on love, or that you've stopped caring. Sometimes, doing nothing is the strongest, clearest, most self-respecting move you've got.

And I know that feels unnatural. Because your instinct, always, has been to do **something**.

You reach out. You repair. You reword the last conversation in your head until it sounds more palatable. You take responsibility for his bad mood because it's easier than sitting with the tension. You draft the follow-up message, the soft clarification, the emotional safety net… again and again, because the discomfort of silence feels unbearable.

You've been taught, by repetition and reward, that love is a performance. That peace is earned through effort. That relationships only survive if someone keeps doing the work, even when the other person has stopped showing up.

And nine times out of ten? That someone has been you.

But here's the paradox: the very thing you think is saving the relationship might be the thing that's suffocating your own healing.

Because every time you fix what he broke, without accountability... every time you re-regulate the emotional temperature of the room so he doesn't have to... every time you step in with one more olive branch, one more explanation, one more "maybe he didn't mean it that way" lifeline — you're not building a bridge. You're building a trap. One that locks **you** in the role of emotional caretaker and lets **him** off the hook, again.

You've done enough.

You've said enough.

You simply stopped abandoning yourself.

And that, love, is everything.

You Don't Need Closure to Choose Freedom

You don't need closure to move on. You don't need the last word. You don't need an apology, an explanation, or a sudden burst of self-awareness from someone who, let's be honest, rarely managed any of that when it actually counted.

You don't need a scene, some cinematic, soul baring conversation where he finally "gets it" and says all the things you've been screaming into the void of your mind for months. That conversation, if it ever comes, usually arrives too late and tells you nothing you didn't already know. And the worst part? You still feel hollow after it. Because closure isn't something he can hand you, it's something you decide to claim, on your own, without his permission, without his understanding, without his emotional signature at the bottom of your healing process. Because **closure is an inside job.**

Closure, as we've been sold it, is a fantasy, one that hinges your peace on someone else's growth, someone else's ability to articulate your pain back to you in a way that makes it all make sense. But if he couldn't hold space for your truth while you were right there in front of him, do you really believe he'll suddenly find the emotional clarity to deliver it after you've already left?

Closure isn't about tying up loose ends with a ribbon. It's about walking away from a tangled mess and choosing not to keep cutting yourself on the knots. It's not a conclusion that gets delivered to your doorstep in a moment of divine synchronicity, it's the choice to stop rereading the last chapter over and over, hoping the words will somehow rearrange into something more comforting.

It's you deciding, in the middle of all the unfinished sentences and unanswered questions, that you don't need a reason to stop bleeding. You just need to stop. You don't need his validation to honor your pain. You don't need a mutual understanding to justify leaving. You don't need the perfect ending to know the story has already run its course.

And yes, **grieving without closure is messy.** It's not the kind of heartbreak you can dress up with a silver lining. It's murky, lonely, and filled with emotional second-guessing. You'll have nights when your brain replays old arguments and tries to rewrite them with a softer tone. You'll wonder if you misread everything. You'll crave one last conversation, not because it would change anything, but because part of you still wants to be seen by someone who never really looked.

But ask yourself this: how much longer are you willing to sit in emotional purgatory, waiting for a man who couldn't give you consistency to now give you clarity? How many more weeks, months, years are you going to spend trying to solve a puzzle that was designed to keep shifting the moment you thought you had it figured out?

Closure isn't a gift he gives you once he's grown enough to understand your worth. It's a boundary you set when you realize you're done teaching someone how to treat you. It's when you choose peace over chaos, even if the peace is quiet, uncertain, and doesn't come with a satisfying narrative arc. It's when you stop reaching back through the wreckage hoping to find something that might finally justify all the pain—and instead, you start reaching forward, toward yourself.

Because the truth is, you were never asking for too much. You were just asking the wrong person.

So, if he never apologizes, **so what?**

If he never acknowledges the damage he caused, **so what?**

If he goes on with his life as if yours wasn't turned upside down…

You still get to walk away.

You still get to heal.

You still get to build something beautiful from the ashes of what never was.

So, let the door stay closed. Let the questions remain unanswered. Let the silence say what his words never could.

Because the moment you stop waiting for closure and start choosing freedom, that's the moment you truly begin.

And that, babe, is the most powerful closure there is.

Breakup Reset: 30-Day No-Contact Protocol

You don't heal by nibbling at the thing that hurt you. You heal by starving the loop that kept you hooked.

For the next 30 days, you're going no contact. Not "mostly." Not "unless he texts." Not "just to drop off his hoodie." Clean. Cold. Complete. That includes your thumbs.

I know it sounds excruciating and nearly impossible right now, but this is medicine, it's not supposed to be tasty.

No contact means:

- No calls, no texts, no DMs, no "accidental" story replies, no late-night "just checking in."

- No checking his socials, his LinkedIn, his new follows, his mother's Facebook, his band's page, or the dog's account… yep, even the dog.

- No rewatching old videos or scrolling those album highlights you curated like a museum.

- No replaying old voicemails "for closure." (They are not closure; they're a nervous-system landmine wrapped in nostalgia.)

- No asking mutual friends for intel, no driving past his street, no "we can still be friends" coffees. You're not friends; you're detoxing.

Why this works (the science, not the slogan):

Your brain is a prediction machine. During the relationship, his voice, his *"hey,"* his blue dot on a map — all of it became **cues** that promised a little dopamine hit, sometimes paired with cortisol and adrenaline when things got chaotic.

That unpredictable mix (high-low, hot-cold) trains the brain through **intermittent reinforcement** — the same schedule that makes slot machines addictive. Every "just a peek" re-fires the loop, strengthens the cue-craving pathway, and drags your body back into fight/flight.

Replaying old voicemails or stalking socials triggers **memory reconsolidation**: when you re-activate a memory, you don't put it back exactly as it was; you re-store it fresher, stickier, more emotionally charged. Translation? One listen = two weeks of healing smudged. No contact removes the cues so your nervous system can **down-regulate**, your reward circuits can **recalibrate**, and the bond can **extinguish** instead of re-ignite.

Make it doable, not heroic:

- **Delete and block.** Everywhere. If you can't trust yourself, have a friend change the passwords on the accounts you spiral on and hold them for 30 days.

- **Box it up.** Phone photos, trinkets, his hoodie: into a literal box, sealed, out of sight. You're not throwing your life away—you're putting the past on ice while your body stabilizes.

- **Choose an accountability human.** One trusted friend who agrees to:

  - check in daily (text or voice),

  - drag you outside in person 2–3x a week (walks, coffee, errands—movement beats rumination),

- hold the line when you wobble (no "maybe just text him" nonsense).

- **Script your urges.** When the itch hits, you don't negotiate with it; you run the script:

    - "This is a craving, not a calling."

    - "In 20 minutes, this wave passes."

    - "I don't feed what I'm trying to starve."

    - Then you **do** something physical for 90 seconds: wall push-ups, brisk stairs, box breathing (4-4-6-2), cold water on wrists—quick body resets that tell your brain, "We're safe."

- **Replace, don't white-knuckle.** Swap scroll time with a set list: grief playlist + shower, neighborhood loop + podcast, meet a friend, journal three pages, cook something crunchy. Boredom is withdrawal, plan for it.

- **Set an emergency plan.** If you slip, you don't spiral, you reset. Text your accountability human one word: "RED." They call you; you hand them your phone for the night; we're done.

Personal Insight: Rewriting the Memories

Here's a little trick I've been using, and it's one of the few breakup tools that actually feels empowering instead of punishing. I call it **rewriting the memories.**

You don't have to burn everything he ever touched or donate half your wardrobe to Goodwill. You can keep the things you love, you just need to **reclaim** them.

Take one item that still buzzes with old association. Maybe it's a top you wore on your first date. A necklace he bought. A song that still stings when it comes on shuffle. Now, instead of exiling it, **re-script it**.

Wear that top somewhere new, like on a trip with friends, at a rooftop bar, somewhere you'll laugh too loud and forget to be haunted. Play that song while you drive with the windows down and someone who makes you feel alive is riding shotgun.

Each time you reintroduce an object or a song or a place into a new, emotionally charged context, your brain re-files the memory. This isn't wishful thinking — **it's neuroscience**.

When a memory is recalled, it briefly becomes malleable, a process known as **memory reconsolidation**. If you pair it with a new, positive emotional experience during that window, your brain **updates the file**. The next time you encounter that cue, it will pull up a different emotional signature — less pain, more power.

So no, you don't have to erase your history to heal from it. You just have to **reclaim the meaning**. That top isn't *"what I wore the night I fell for him."* It's ***"what I wore the night I remembered who I am."***

What you can expect:

- Day 1–5: Noise. Urges. Muscle memory reaching for your phone. This is withdrawal, not a sign to turn back.

- Day 6–14: Fog lifts in slices. Sleep improves. Random waves still punch at 2 p.m. — ride them, don't read them.

- Day 15–30: Your body starts believing you. Less checking, more appetite, more laughter that doesn't feel borrowed.

After 30 days:

Re-evaluate from your **center**, not your craving. You are not reopening the loop; you're deciding, clear-eyed, what supports your peace. If you still want contact, ask: *"Does this move me toward healing or toward history?"* If it's the latter, extend another 30 days. Your peace isn't on a deadline.

Neuroscience research backs this up: **most people need roughly 90 days for their neural pathways to start rewiring after a deep emotional attachment.**

That's how long it typically takes for the reward circuits, stress hormones, and memory networks to calm down enough that your brain stops treating the absence of the person as a literal threat. In other words, 30 days gets you out of the emergency room. Ninety days rewires the system.

So, no contact isn't cruelty, it's rehabilitation. You're letting your nervous system **down-regulate**, your reward circuits **recalibrate**, and your bond **extinguish** instead of re-ignite.

CHAPTER 8:

THE BREAKUP THAT HAPPENS IN YOUR HEAD

Just Because He Couldn't Love You Fully Doesn't Mean You Were Hard to Love

After the dust settles, after the final argument, after the last time you gave him a chance to show up and he still didn't, that's when it hits you in the quiet:

He just couldn't love you the way you needed to be loved.

And that truth lands heavy, even when it's clean. Because maybe you're not crying anymore. Maybe you've stopped checking your phone. Maybe you've even started sleeping through the night again. But there's still that whisper in the back of your mind asking, *"Was I too much?"*

Let me stop you right there.

No, you weren't too much.

You were too **aware**. Too **accountable**. Too **clear-eyed** about what partnership actually means.

You were someone who saw what needed to be done and got tired of carrying all of it alone.

And maybe he loved you in his own way. But love that leaves you over-functioning, second-guessing, and emotionally malnourished? That's not love. That's survival with good intentions.

But here's the truth: he didn't fall short because you were hard to love.

He fell short because he wasn't capable of loving you in a grown-ass, sustainable, reciprocal way.

So let this be your unlearning:

- You weren't too intense. You were deeply present.

- You weren't too demanding. You had actual standards.

- You weren't "cold" for walking away. You were on fire, and he didn't even bring water.

You gave him the chance to meet you where you were.

He stayed sitting on the curb.

That's not rejection. That's a reflection. Of him. Not you.

Let him go. Let the story go.

You don't need to rewrite what happened to make it make sense.

You just need to remember: **the right love won't ask you to disappear to keep it.**

His Emotional Limitations Aren't Proof of Your Unworthiness

When someone keeps failing to love you the way you need, it's easy to turn their emotional incompetence into your personal indictment. You don't mean to do it. But after the third or fourth letdown, you stop asking, *"Why can't he meet me here?"* and you start wondering, *"What's wrong with me that I keep asking?"*

You think, *maybe I'm too sensitive. Too intense. Too deep. Too much.*

Or worse—*maybe I'm just not worth that kind of love.*

And babe, I need you to hear this like it's a sermon from your future self:

His emotional limitations are not a mirror of your worth.

They are his.

His upbringing. His trauma. His avoidance. His choices.

His inability to communicate clearly, hold space for you, take accountability, or emotionally show up on a consistent basis — **none of that is about you.**

You just happened to be the one holding out your heart while he kept fumbling the handoff.

It's not your fault he was emotionally under-equipped.

It's not your job to become smaller, quieter, less "demanding" just to fit inside the cramped emotional bandwidth he was willing to offer.

And it's definitely not your destiny to carry the weight of someone else's healing just so you can **earn** the bare minimum.

His inconsistency didn't mean you were hard to love.

It meant he had no idea how to love **consistently**.

His defensiveness wasn't because you were being "critical."

It's because he heard truth as an attack.

His shutdowns weren't caused by your tone.

They were just his go-to when shit got real.

You probably bent over backwards trying to "say it better," "be softer," "meet him where he's at." You went to emotional grad school while he was still skipping intro class. And still… nothing changed. Not really. Not sustainably. Because it wasn't your delivery. It was his inability.

So, let's untangle this right now.

- He didn't pull away because you were unlovable.

- He pulled away because closeness asked him to grow.

- He didn't stonewall because you were hysterical.

- He stonewalled because your vulnerability terrified him.

- He didn't change because he couldn't? Maybe.

- Or because he wouldn't? That's the part that matters.

Either way, it has **zero** to do with your worth.

You were always worthy of being met. Of being heard. Of being loved out loud by someone who wasn't intimidated by your emotional clarity but attracted to it. Someone who sees your depth not as a threat, but as the very reason they want to stay.

You don't have to shrink to be loved.

You don't have to be less just to be chosen.

The right person won't make you second-guess the very things that make you whole.

So, when someone keeps proving that they **can't** show up for you emotionally, don't take that as a sign to dim your light. Take it as a sign that they were never equipped to walk beside it in the first place.

Boundaries As Self-Respect

You Didn't Fail the Relationship, You Honored It by Being Honest

There's this quiet, corrosive myth that so many of us carry — one that wraps around the heart like a guilt-laced vine and whispers, again and again, that if the **relationship ended, it meant you failed.** That if it didn't last, it wasn't love. That if you couldn't hold it together until the end of time, then somehow you weren't strong enough, patient enough, forgiving enough, woman enough.

And so, you sit with that heaviness, turning over every conversation like a post-mortem, wondering what more you could've done, how much longer you could've stayed, or whether the version of you who finally left was just a coward in disguise.

But the truth, the real, raw, unsentimental truth is this: **sometimes the most loving thing you can do is walk away before the damage becomes permanent.** Sometimes honesty doesn't look like one more fight or another desperate attempt to make it work. Sometimes it looks like a soft, quiet line drawn in the sand that says, *"I've reached the edge of myself, and I refuse to go any further into this emptiness pretending it's connection."*

So, no. You didn't fail the relationship, you stayed longer than most would have. You showed up on days you had nothing left in the tank. You opened your heart when it would've been easier to shut down. You listened. You explained. You softened, adjusted, forgave, and made room again and again for a version of him you kept hoping would finally meet you where you were. You shaped yourself into a hundred different silhouettes trying to fit a mold that never existed. And when it still didn't work, not because of a lack of love but because of a lack of mutual growth, you did the bravest thing you've ever done — you told the truth.

The kind of truth that rises up slowly, steadily, like a tide, until you can't deny it anymore. The kind that says, *"I can love you and still leave. I can care deeply and still choose myself. I can grieve what we had and still know, deep in my bones, that this can't be my home anymore."*

That's integrity. That's choosing clarity over comfort, peace over the illusion of harmony, truth over the safety of denial.

You stopped sacrificing your dignity on the altar of potential. And maybe he'll never see that. Maybe he'll tell himself a story where you were the one who walked away too soon, or stopped loving too fast, or didn't try hard enough. But that's his narrative to carry. You don't owe it space in your chest.

Because what you did was courage.

So no, you didn't fail.

You told the truth.

And the truth — however hard, however final — is a form of love too.

Real Boundaries Protect Connection *With Yourself,* Not Just Others

Boundaries aren't walls you build to keep people out, they're anchors you drop to keep from drifting so far from yourself you don't even recognize who's staring back in the mirror anymore. They're about staying tethered to your own worth when everything around you, especially the person you're with, keeps tugging at your edges and testing how far you'll bend before you break.

Because when you're in a relationship that slowly, almost imperceptibly, erodes your self-respect, your focus shifts. You start thinking boundaries are there to preserve the peace between you and him. You frame it like diplomacy. You tell yourself you're trying to "keep the connection intact." But the truth is, every time you say *"it's fine"* when your stomach's in knots, every time you downplay your needs to avoid looking needy, every time you rewrite your truth to make it more palatable — you're not protecting the relationship. You're sacrificing yourself to keep the illusion alive.

And eventually? That costs you more than it saves.

Real boundaries are the line in the sand that says, *"I still love you, but I love myself more than I fear your discomfort."*

And no, you don't need to make a scene or hand out laminated flashcards every time you draw one. Boundaries don't always come with big announcements or carefully worded speeches. Sometimes they sound like, *"I'm not explaining this again."* Sometimes they look like you going quiet, not out of fear, but because repeating yourself would only drain you further. Sometimes it's a look, a pause, a door left gently closed because staying would've meant losing one more piece of yourself.

A boundary is more of a mirror than a threat. One that reflects who you are and what you will and will not negotiate anymore.

It's about committing to your own integrity, even if they flinch, pout, lash out, or leave. That's you learning, maybe for the first time, that connection without self-abandonment isn't just possible, it's required.

That's the real kind of connection—the one with yourself—that will never ask you to shrink in order to belong.

Saying "No More" Is How You Make Space for Real Peace

There's a shift that happens so quietly, you almost miss it. This deep, visceral knowing that rolls through your body like thunder in your bones: **I'm done.** Not "maybe." Not "let's see how it goes." Not "I'll wait one more week." Just done.

Your lips might not even say the words, but your nervous system screams them loud and clear. And when that moment comes, it's not because you're cruel, impatient, or unforgiving, it's because you've finally remembered your worth.

That internal **no more** doesn't need to be explained or defended. It doesn't come from bitterness. It's born from clarity. Clarity that whispers, *"I have bent, compromised, over-functioned, and contorted myself into every possible shape to keep something alive that keeps draining me in return."* You reach a point where loving him feels like losing you. And when that realization hits, peace becomes non-negotiable.

"No more" is not about slamming doors, it's about closing the ones that keep letting chaos walk in like it pays rent. It's about sealing the cracks where your self-worth has been leaking out in the form of over-explaining, second chances, and bending over backwards for someone who won't even meet you halfway. It's not a rage-fueled exit. It's not a mic drop. It's a stillness. Heavy, dark and inevitable. You can almost hear thunder rolling in the distance, and you know that it's the pain knocking on your door, but you also know there's a rainbow on the other side of that storm, and quiet, and peace.

Real peace sometimes looks like being alone on a Friday night and realizing your body isn't clenched in defense. Sometimes it's silence — thick, undramatic, beautiful silence. Sometimes it's waking up in a bed where no one's snoring beside you, no one's sulking in the kitchen, and no one's making you question if today will be another empty lonely day with a crowded calendar.

Sometimes peace is discipline. Sometimes peace is deletion. Sometimes peace is blocking his number with zero ceremony and lighting a candle.

You don't say "no more" because you stopped loving. You say it because you started listening — to your gut, to your fatigue, to the small, quiet voice that's been whispering for months, "This isn't it."

So, say it, maybe not out loud, maybe not to him, but to yourself. Say it in a journal. Say it in your sleep. Say it in the shower while you scrub off the residue of all the times you settled. Say it in a way you don't respond. Say it in a way you reclaim your time.

No more.

That's your spell. Your shield. Your exit key. And the space it opens up is a sanctuary.

Guard it. Guard it like the whole f*king universe depends on it!

You Can Release Without Bitterness

Letting Go Is Sacred and Sometimes Ugly

There's this quiet, almost reverent kind of grief that hits you when you finally realize you're not going back, simply because the version of you that kept holding on doesn't exist anymore. And what replaces her is clarity. A kind of bone-deep knowing that love, no matter how deep it once was, cannot survive on one person's willingness to carry the whole thing.

You can still miss him. You can still feel your chest tighten when that one song plays or when your body instinctively reaches for the shape of him in bed before your mind remembers he's not there. You can remember the good mornings, the inside jokes, the way he used to look at you like you hung the moon — and none of that has to mean you made the wrong decision.

Maybe he wasn't malicious. Maybe he really did love you, in the way he was capable of. Maybe he tried — half-heartedly, inconsistently, with no tools or staying power, but maybe he did try. And maybe it still wasn't enough. Maybe you needed more than he could offer. And maybe that's not a crime but just a truth.

That truth can live quietly in your chest like a gentle ache that slowly turns into wisdom. Because you don't need to hate someone to walk away. You don't need rage to fuel your exit. You just need to trust that what you wanted — mutuality, emotional maturity, presence, partnership, was never actually on the table, no matter how many pretty words were spoken or how hard you squinted to see potential where there was only pattern.

You can still care about him, want the best for him, still hope he gets his shit together one day, just not at the cost of your peace, not at the expense of your future, not while standing in the wreckage of your own needs waiting for him to grow.

And closure... closure sometimes shows up in your kitchen on a random Tuesday, in the stillness of not checking your phone, in the ease of making coffee for one without feeling the weight of disappointment sitting across from you. Sometimes closure is just a deep breath followed by the soft but steady thought: **I'm done.**

Forgiveness Is Optional. Peace Is Not.

Forgiveness is not a requirement, not a rite of passage. It's not the magical final boss you have to defeat before you're allowed to heal. It's just one path. Not the only one, one of many. And despite what every yoga-flavored Instagram quote wants you to believe, you're allowed to walk away with your dignity intact and your forgiveness... unoffered.

Because peace? Peace just needs you to stop bleeding energy into something that already took more than its share.

You can still be angry. You can still feel it in your body when his name comes up. You can flinch at the memory, wince at the songs, and shake your head when people say, *"He meant well."* Maybe he did. Maybe he didn't. Doesn't matter. **The damage was done.**

And your job now is to walk away from the wreckage and stop trying to organize it into something workable.

You can say, *I don't forgive you* — and still be free.

You can say, *I'm not over it yet* — and still move forward.

You can say, *I'm done carrying this* — and set it down without a single ounce of grace toward the person who dropped it in your lap in the first place.

Forgiveness is personal. But peace? **Peace is non-negotiable.** You don't need to be the bigger person. You just need to stop letting what happened keep writing the story of what comes next.

And you don't need a final conversation to make your departure real. You don't need his comprehension to make your clarity valid. You don't need to explain your boundary for the seventh time and call it "closure."

You already **closed it.** The moment you stopped pleading. The moment you packed your peace and walked out without slamming the door, because you didn't need to.

You were the ending.

You were the clarity.

You were the last damn line.

Closure is the moment you realize that no matter how many drafts you write in your head, there's no version where he magically becomes the man you needed. There's no final monologue. No teary reunion. No cinematic redemption arc. Just you, breathing for the first time without waiting for someone else to catch up.

You are the final word. Full stop. No edits. No encore.

Scene's over.

Curtain.

CHAPTER 9:

WHEN WALKING ALONE STARTS TO FEEL LIGHTER

Returning to Yourself

Waking Up Is Brutal

You don't wake up one morning, stretch your arms, smile at the sunrise, and whisper, *"I deserve better."* Nope. You wake up like someone just ripped the f*cking blindfold off after years of calling it a scarf. Your eyes sting. Your chest aches. And the first thing you feel isn't freedom, it's nausea, anvil in the chest and a brain fog.

Because when the real truth finally lands, the kind that's been circling overhead for months, maybe years — it doesn't show up with confetti and clarity, it hits like a quiet punch to the gut. It's you sitting in your car in some random parking lot, staring at the steering wheel and realizing, *"Oh my god… this is never going to change."* And then you cry. Not because you're weak, but because your nervous system is finally catching up to what your intuition knew three breakdowns ago.

I remember sitting in my apartment the first night after I left. No shouting. No eggshells. No wondering if my tone would ruin the evening. And you know what I felt? Not peace. Not power. Just… dread. My nervous system didn't know what to do without the adrenaline. I wasn't free, I was twitchy, restless, craving the next emotional spike just to feel alive again. It took me weeks to realize that what I was missing wasn't love. It was survival chemistry. And it was f*cking up my ability to trust calm.

And waking up hurt like hell, because it meant I couldn't unknow what I knew. You can't un-feel how small you had to make yourself just to keep things from unraveling. You can't un-see how often you silenced your gut to keep the peace. You can't unknow that you became someone you don't even recognize anymore — just to hold it all together.

And honestly, the holding together was Olympic-level. Just like me, you were out here doing full-time emotional labor with no holidays, no hazard pay, and no damn support team. Therapist, translator, crisis management, bedtime clown — whatever was needed. You didn't just bend. You **folded**. You contorted yourself into the shape of "maybe this time it'll be enough."

But it never was, was it?

You kept hoping the potential you saw in him would eventually catch up to the person in front of you. That maybe, just maybe, he'd look up one day and realize what he had. That the love you were pouring — shit, **funneling** — into him would eventually soak through. That he'd grow. Evolve. Snap out of it. Remember your birthday without prompting. Read a goddamn book. Feel remorse. Anything.

But all he ever did was get better at surviving your disappointment. And you? You got better at pretending it didn't hurt.

Until one day, something cracked. Not loud. Not dramatic. Just… cracked. Maybe it was something stupid, like him forgetting the groceries **again**. Or brushing off your sadness with a half-assed joke. Or asking what's wrong and then checking his phone halfway through your answer. But this time, something in you didn't smooth it over. You just **saw** it. Clear as glass. Clear as, *"I cannot do this one more time without losing whatever's left of me."*

And that clarity came with grief.

Because you **can** love someone and still know they are not your person.

You can remember the good and still recognize that the bad was what you carried alone.

You can cry your f*cking eyes out on the bathroom floor and still know, deep in your bones, that staying would be a bigger betrayal than leaving.

Waking up is not some goddess moment where you float out the door in a satin robe whispering affirmations. It's messy. It's devastating. It's sobbing into a takeout container while re-reading texts that felt magical three months ago and now make you sick to your stomach.

But it's also the beginning. Not of healing, not yet. But of truth.

And truth, baby, is holy.

It doesn't always feel good. But it will **save your life**.

It's Not Weak to Miss Him. It's Human

No one tells you that freedom can feel like falling at first.

You just sit there confused, disoriented, like a bloody deer in the head-lights, trying to decide what to do next to feel normal, comfortable again.

Because sure, walking away sounds brave… bold, even. But let's not bullshit ourselves: being alone after a relationship, even a dysfunctional, soul-draining one, can be f*cking terrifying.

The Bed Still Smells Like Him

Maybe the first night, maybe the fifth, you will roll over and reach for someone who isn't there… and that's when it hits. Not just the absence of his body, but the weight of everything that used to fill that space. His breath. His warmth. His silence when you needed comfort. His back turned to you after an argument you tried your best to solve before it got ugly.

The bed is quiet now. But it's not peaceful yet. Not at first. It's loud with everything you swallowed for too long.

And the world, your friends, the podcasts, the books, will tell you this part is supposed to feel empowering. They'll say, *"Isn't it amazing? You've got the whole bed to yourself!"* And sure, maybe one day you'll starfish across those sheets like the goddess you are. But tonight? Tonight you're curled up on the edge like a goddamn question mark, wondering **how something so necessary can feel so unbearable.**

Because no one talks about how grief shows up in stupid, cruel ways. Like in the middle of the night when a song lyric knocks the wind out of you. Or when you instinctively go to text him that something funny just happened, before you remember you're not talking anymore. Before you remember that this distance wasn't created by accident. That you chose it. That you had to.

And that's what makes it so excruciating.

Because it wasn't all bad. If it was, this would be easy. If he was a total asshole every second of every day, you could just burn it down and never look back. But he wasn't. There were moments, real ones, that felt like love. And that's what keeps you up at night. That's what haunts the empty side of the bed. Not just the loss of him, but the loss of who you were trying to be when you still believed it could work.

You miss the idea more than the man.

You miss the fantasy more than the fight.

You miss having someone to hold, even if you were the only one doing the holding.

And that's the part you don't admit out loud, right? That even when the relationship was draining you, leaving still cracked something open inside you so wide you could barely breathe. Because it meant facing every version of yourself you kept buried under the "we." The woman who tolerated. The woman who hoped. The woman who dimmed. The woman who gave and gave and called it strength, when really? She was just f*cking exhausted.

So yeah, the empty bed hurts. It stings like hell. And maybe you cry into a pillow that still smells like him, or maybe you rip the sheets off and wash them three times in one night, desperate to scrub the history out of the fibers. There's no rulebook for this part. Just you. And your breath. And the hollow place where the future you imagined used to sleep.

But here's the truth buried under all that pain: this emptiness **is your threshold.**

It's the doorway between what you survived and what you're about to become.

And yeah, tonight it feels like loss.

But one day… maybe not soon, maybe not cleanly — you'll realize it was the first night you finally got to sleep in a bed that belongs to just you.

Your bed. Your rules. Your peace.

Even if right now it still hurts like a skinny dip in the acid.

No one tells you how loud it gets after the noise leaves

You'd think silence would be soft. Gentle. A reprieve. But when you've spent years filling your life with the static of someone else's moods, apologies, deflections, and long-ass explanations that never actually explained anything — it's the silence that finally hits the hardest.

Because now it's just you. No one to decode. No one to fix. No emotional landmines to step around. And somehow… that's terrifying.

There's no script for this part, either. No comforting background hum of "we" to drown out the ache of "me." The TV doesn't help. The music doesn't help. Even your thoughts don't feel like yours yet — they still echo with his voice, his opinions, the way he'd twist your words until you weren't sure if you were crazy or just exhausted. You were always explaining yourself. Always adjusting the temperature of the room so he wouldn't shut down or blow up or sulk into the next day. And now? Now, the room is still.

And that stillness feels dangerous at first.

You start to realize how much you relied on chaos to feel alive. How the rollercoaster of "Are we okay?" became your emotional baseline. How your body only knows how to tense. To brace. To respond. You don't even know what calm feels like yet, you just know it feels unfamiliar. Suspicious, even. Like something must be wrong if there isn't a crisis to manage or a conversation to rehearse for the seventh time in your head.

But here's the thing about that silence: **it's not empty. It's sacred**.

It's the sound of you coming back to yourself.

It's the moment when your nervous system finally starts to uncoil after being in fight-or-f*cking-flight for years. It's when the screaming quiets down, the sound of your own damn voice rising up again, shaky at first, then steady, then so goddamn clear it stuns you. Because underneath all the noise you absorbed, all the bullshit you tolerated, all the over-explaining and over-performing and over-giving — you're still here.

Still breathing. Still yours.

And sure, it's lonely. Of course it is. You miss the illusion of connection. The false comfort of a body next to yours while your heart sat in exile. You miss feeling wanted, even if it was conditional. You miss the routine, even if it was draining the life out of you. But this silence? This is the part where you stop performing. Where you stop translating your worth into actions someone else barely noticed. Where you sit in the stillness and, for the first time in a long time, ask: what do **I** need?

Not what will keep him calm.

Not what will keep the peace.

What do I need?

And you might not know the answer yet. That's okay. The silence will teach you. If you let it. If you stop trying to outrun it with distractions and numbing and pretending you're fine. You don't have to be fine. You just have to be honest.

Real peace doesn't come wrapped in a bow. It doesn't walk in loud and proud with a spotlight. It tiptoes in through the silence. Through the ache. Through the moments you sit with your own damn self and say, *"Okay. So, this is what it feels like to not be lied to anymore."*

It's raw. It's real. And yeah, it's f*cking uncomfortable.

But it's also the beginning of everything you forgot you were allowed to feel.

It's Not Him You Miss

This part right here? This is where most women slide back into that black hole of "maybe it wasn't that bad." This is where your brain starts running highlight reels of the two good weeks he was emotionally available, spliced together with that one time he picked up dinner without being asked, and suddenly you're staring at your phone like it's an Ouija board, waiting for his name to flicker back into your notifications like a ghost you swore you buried.

But what you're actually missing isn't him. **It's the version of him you built in your head.**

You miss who he **could've** been. Who he **promised** he might become. Who he **showed you** in just enough glimpses to keep you hooked.

You're not grieving reality, you're grieving illusion. A relationship built on maybes and crumbs and "if only"s that you dressed up in hope.

You miss the way it felt when he was present, not the way it felt when he disappeared into silence or sarcasm or cold detachment for days on end. You miss the way your body relaxed during those rare moments he actually showed up with softness, not the way your gut twisted every time you brought up something vulnerable and watched it bounce off him like a bloody tennis ball.

Because the truth is, the man you loved **only existed sometimes**. And those sometimes were **just** frequent enough to make you question your standards and silence your gut. Just enough to make you rewrite the story in your head: *"He's just stressed. He didn't mean it like that. Maybe I was too sensitive."*

No, babe. You were spot on. You just didn't want to be.

So yeah, cry for the dream.

Cry for the version of him that felt like home when you needed shelter.

Cry for the story you tried to write together, even if he never picked up the pen.

And then remind yourself: **what you're missing isn't real.** It **felt** real but it never was. It was stitched together with your labor, your patience, your imagination, your love holding both ends of a rope he never bothered to grip.

And in that space where the fantasy dies?

You get yourself back.

When He Texts, and You Almost Fold

(The moment your nervous system betrays your better judgment)

There's that split second. You know the one.

You're fine. You're doing your thing. Maybe you're cleaning the kitchen. Maybe you're out getting your shit together. Maybe you finally had a whole day where you didn't think about him.

And then... **ping**.

The name flashes.

Your stomach drops.

Your body reacts before your brain does.

Suddenly your hands are shaking and you're rereading the message like it's written in some dead language you forgot how to speak.

"I miss u."

That's it. Three words. Not even spelled properly. But they hit like a f*cking freight train.

And no matter how much work you've done, how clear your decision was, how many damn journal entries you wrote about why you had to leave — it still gets you. Because for a second, it feels like maybe he finally sees it. Maybe he gets what he lost. Maybe this time will be different.

But let's be honest.

What you're craving isn't him.

It's **relief**.

From the silence. From the loneliness. From carrying the memory of a man who, for a while, felt like home, even if that home had mold in the walls and a gas leak you kept pretending didn't smell.

Your body isn't stupid. It remembers the dopamine. It remembers the laugh, the in-jokes, the way it felt when you were wanted, even if that want came with conditions. Even if it hurt.

And so now, standing there with your phone in your hand and your hope crawling up your throat like it never f*cking left, you feel it: the urge to reply. To crack the door. To let a little air back in, even if it reeks of the same old smoke.

But wait.

Before you hit *"I miss you too"*

Stop.

This is your trauma bond doing a karaoke cover of Adele at 2AM.

You don't owe your peace to a man who only finds his feelings after you walk away.

You don't owe access to someone who only wants you when you're gone.

You don't need to go back just to double-check that it still hurts.

So, here's your **Stay-Strong Strategy** — the emergency plan for when your chest is tight, your eyes are glassy, and your lonely is louder than your logic:

1. Don't respond. Not yet. Not now.

You are not a reflex. You are not a reply button. Put the phone down. Walk away from the dopamine slot machine.

2. Say this out loud:

"This is a trigger. Not a sign. Not a soulmate. Not a sign from the universe. A. F*cking. Trigger."

Let the words sound bitter in your mouth if they need to. That bitterness? It's better than regret.

3. Breathe.

Box breathing. In for 4, hold for 4, out for 6. Again. Feel your feet on the floor. You are here. Not there. Not in the past.

4. Grab your receipts.

Go back to your journal, your notes app, your "I Will Not Settle for Less Than This" list. The one you wrote on the day you swore never again. Let her speak to you now. Let her remind you why you left. Why you cried. Why you almost lost yourself.

5. If you absolutely must reply, do it from your healed self, not your lonely one.

Try this:

"I've worked too hard to come back to a version of me I've already buried. I wish you well. Please don't contact me again."

Still feel harsh? Then remind yourself:

You are not being cruel. You are being clear.

You don't need to let him re-enter your life just because he finally noticed the door was closed.

Listen, I know.

I know the nights get cold, I know the bed feels empty and the memories feel softer than the reality ever was.

But girl, **you are not cold. You are finally clear.**

So, when that message lands, and your chest caves for just a second, and your brain starts running all the what-ifs like a reel you didn't ask for — **Don't move. Don't reply. Don't reach.**

Yet still there's that part of you — small, sharp, stubborn — that still wants to follow up just to say you **don't** care.

Just to prove you've won the detachment war.

It's ridiculous, right?

You've blocked him. You've worked your way to clarity. You've read every damn quote about healing and heartbreak. And yet…

Now you desperately want him to know how indifferent you are. Sounds like an oxymoron, doesn't it?

That isn't closure, sis. That's ego, still waiting for applause, the wound, dressed in lipstick, hoping he notices the scar and flinches.

You don't owe him your progress packaged as performance.

Not answering is what makes it real.

You don't need to clap back with a clever line. You don't need to prove how unfazed you are. You've already done the most radical thing a woman can do after surviving emotional depletion: you chose to stop engaging.

And sometimes, **not replying is the loudest thing** you'll ever say.

Walking Away Doesn't Mean You Wanted To

You're Allowed to Miss Him and Still Not Want Him Back

Some nights, the missing hits you sideways. Just because your body hasn't caught up to your decision yet.

And that's the brutal, beautiful contradiction of grief: it doesn't wait for logic. It doesn't care that you wrote the pros and cons list, had the therapy sessions, said the big goodbye. It doesn't care that you **know** he wasn't good for you. That your nervous system is finally unclenching, that you're waking up without dread pressing down on your chest. No, grief shows up anyway. Like a ghost with good timing. It curls up next to you when the house goes quiet on a Sunday night and your hands have nothing to do but feel.

And you start missing him. The way his voice used to dip when he was tired. The lines around his eyes when he smiled. His voice. The stupid way he stirred his coffee… Missing just a **proof you had the guts to walk away from something you once deeply wanted.** You mourn because it mattered. Because you cared. Because your love was real, even if the relationship couldn't carry it.

And you know what? That ache in your chest? It means you're human. It means you're healing. It means your heart is recalibrating after being stretched too far for too long.

Missing is not the same as needing or settling. It is not a summons to self-abandon.

You can miss him… and still remember all the times you cried yourself to sleep.

You can miss him... and still know he made you question your worth more than he ever reflected it back to you.

You can miss him... and still choose your peace over another ride on the apology carousel.

You're allowed to have both truths in your mouth at once.

"I loved him." **and** *"I'm still leaving."*

This isn't about erasing the good. This is about refusing to use the good as a reason to keep swallowing the bad. You're not heartless. You're just finally listening to the parts of you that were whispering *"this hurts"* while everyone else kept telling you to hold on.

You don't need to defend your sadness. And you sure as hell don't need to translate it into action. Just feel it. Cry if you need to. Sit in it like the sacred space it is. Then remind yourself, again and again: **Missing him doesn't mean he belonged in your future. It just means he was part of your past.** And that's allowed.

You can miss someone and still not open the door.

You can love someone and still know they weren't safe to stay with.

You can ache... and still keep walking.

Yes, loneliness hurts. But it's an honest pain. It doesn't gaslight you. It doesn't shift the blame. It doesn't tell you you're too much, too sensitive, too needy, too demanding. It just sits beside you. It just asks to be witnessed. And when you let it be what it is — not a sign you messed up, not a punishment, but a byproduct of choosing yourself — you'll start to feel something underneath it.

Not joy. Not yet.

But something like... oxygen?..

Something like peace, learning how to take up space in your body again. As if your nervous system learning it doesn't have to brace every time the door opens.

You know that staying would've broken you. Not all at once. Not in a dramatic movie scene. But slowly, insidiously. Death by 1000 cuts. Through the thousand tiny moments of self-abandonment that you were getting way too good at normalizing. Through the way your laughter got quieter, your body got tighter, your eyes stopped lighting up when you talked about the future. Through the way you were starting to forget who you were before you became a full-time emotional manager with no pay and no damn days off.

You miss him? Fine. You miss the feeling of being held, of having a warm body nearby? Totally human. But remember this: you were lonelier in that relationship than you are now in this bed alone.

You just didn't have time to feel it then, you were too busy managing **his** feelings. Now, finally, you've got space to feel your own.

So, feel it now. Cry into the pillow. Hug yourself like it's the only pair of arms available tonight, because it is. And it's enough. For now.

Then a little longer, then maybe for some time after that..

And then a little longer…

And then something shifts.

It's subtle. Doesn't announce itself. There are no fanfares, no "you made it" banner draped across your wall. Just a moment, on a Tuesday maybe, when you realize you've made your coffee exactly how you like it, and there's no one around to screw it up or leave the mug half-full on the table. A moment when your shoulders drop and you exhale, and it hits you: **this is mine**. This peace, this space, this life. It belongs to you again.

You finally started remembering how to love yourself in daylight.

Solitude used to feel like exile. Like the penalty box for women who stopped tolerating crumbs. But now? Now it's starting to feel like clean air. Like room to stretch. Like that quiet moment before dawn when the world hasn't decided who it's going to be yet… and you haven't either.

There are still echoes. Still nights when the bed feels too big and the silence feels too personal. But those echoes don't hurt the same way anymore. They don't scream "you're unlovable." They whisper something else entirely: **you're free**.

You don't have to prove anything in this space. You don't have to explain your tone or tiptoe around someone else's volatility or emotionally babysit a man-child who calls it love. You don't have to justify why you're tired, or ask permission to rest. You just get to be. Messy, brilliant, broken, healing — you, as you are. And for the first time in too damn long, that's enough.

And maybe that's what this whole chapter has been about. Not the grief, not the heartbreak, not even the leaving, but the returning. To yourself.

And now, as you stand in this quiet, sacred in-between, you get to ask a different question.

Not *"Will I be okay?"*

But ***"What kind of life do I want now where I'm no longer shrinking to survive someone else's?"***

And that question?

That's where Part IV begins.

PART IV:

YOUR COME-BACK ERA STARTS NOW

And here you are.

Maybe you feel lighter. Maybe you feel like you can finally breathe again. Or maybe you're scared shitless and wondering, *What the hell happens now?*

This is what happens now: **you rebuild.**

No Pinterest quotes and empty affirmations, but rituals, systems, standards, and choices that are aligned with the woman you're becoming. Because if I was the voice in your head when you left, then I'm not leaving you now. I'm not handing you a pep talk and disappearing.

This part of the book is where I set you up to actually **live the life** that peace promised you.

No fluff. No shame. No unrealistic "you got this, queen" garbage.

Just clear tools, real talk, and next steps that keep you grounded when doubt creeps in, and focused when your old patterns come knocking.

You made the hard call. You chose yourself.

Now it's time to **build a life that backs that choice up**.

So, thank you for trusting me!

Hold on to your knickers, girl! Let's begin.

CHAPTER 10:

THE WHY: NEUROSCIENCE OF EMOTIONAL HUNGER

The Rubber Band Theory

There's always been a part of me that knew this wasn't healthy. That it's not "normal" to feel physically unwell because he didn't text back for six hours. That it shouldn't feel like a tidal wave of panic every time he needs space. But try telling that to my nervous system, the same one that reacts like a damn fire alarm every time I feel even a little ignored.

Here's what it feels like: there's an invisible rubber band stretched between me and him. When we're close, it's loose, easy, even comforting. But the minute the distance creeps in, emotional or physical, it starts to pull. The further away he drifts, the tighter it stretches. And eventually, it burns. That ache and tightness in your chest? That racing mind? That compulsive need to "just check in"? That's not just insecurity. That's your body **screaming for connection** the only way it knows how: by gripping, chasing, bending until you almost snap.

And let me be real with you: I didn't invent this metaphor because it sounded poetic. **I lived it.** I still do sometimes.

This isn't just "attachment style" fluff on TikTok. This is your nervous system, shaped by experiences that were probably never your fault — like emotional neglect, inconsistent care, or straight-up abandonment when you were too young to even name what was happening. Your brain learned early: closeness equals safety, distance equals threat. So now you **crave closeness like oxygen**, and when it's missing, even a little, you spiral.

And maybe you've been told you're "too intense," "too sensitive," "too needy." But what no one talks about is how much goddamn effort it takes to **not** act on that craving. To let the text go unanswered. To stop yourself from crafting three different versions of *"Just thinking of you :)"* that you never send. To stay put and not chase.

Because if you've ever felt this, you know it's not about him. It's not even about this one relationship. It's about **every freakin' time you were left waiting**. Every time your needs were too big, too loud, too inconvenient. Every time you had to manage your own emotions because no one else knew how. This need for closeness? It's a survival strategy your inner child duct-taped together to avoid falling apart. And now it runs the show.

You might even live with your partner, see him every bloody day, and **still** feel this ache. Because this isn't about physical distance, it's about emotional attunement. You can be in the same room and still feel miles apart. You can be touched and still starved. And if he's checked out, emotionally unavailable, or just inconsistent, you feel it like a punch to the chest.

So, if you've ever asked yourself, *"Why does it hurt so bad for seemingly no reason?"* — here's your answer: **because your nervous system is wired to treat emotional distance like a red alarm emergency.**

And listen, you're not crazy or weak or broken.

You're responding exactly how your body learned to respond when connection felt fragile or conditional.

This is the raw, biological truth:

- Your brain developed in a way that over-prioritizes closeness to soothe threat.

- Your stress response flares up not just from danger, but from perceived disconnection.

- Your hormones, especially cortisol and oxytocin, go haywire when attachment feels insecure.

This is why you bend. This is why you overgive, shape-shift, hyper-function, and carry the relationship on your back just to feel close again.

And now for the real twist: You can love someone deeply and still be reenacting an old wound. You can chase someone who's emotionally unavailable and convince yourself it's passion, not panic. You can think you're fighting for the relationship… when really, you're just fighting to not be left behind. Again.

So, what do we do with this?

First, **we name it.**

Then we start to **interrupt it**, not shame it. Not muscle through it. Interrupt it with compassion and strategy.

You don't have to throw yourself into cold detachment. You just have to start noticing the pattern and choosing differently. You don't have to stop wanting connection, but you **do** have to stop buying it with self-abandonment.

And this is why the next section matters. Because we're not just diving into why this shows up in **you,** we're about to look at why it shows up in **him,** too.

Because the rubber band doesn't just stretch one way.

Why He's Avoiding the Very Thing You're Starving For

While you're gripping that rubber band for dear life, he might be doing everything he can to loosen it. Not because he doesn't love you. But because **emotional closeness doesn't feel safe to him,** it feels suffocating.

You're chasing connection to feel secure, and he's dodging it to feel free. Same relationship. Two nervous systems screaming in opposite languages.

Let's break it down.

If you were raised to equate connection with survival, he may have been raised to equate **connection with control**. Maybe love in his world came with strings. Expectations. Pressure. Or worse — manipulation, shame or punishment. So, his brain clocked vulnerability as dangerous. He learned that if he opened up, he'd lose autonomy, be judged, or get hurt. And now, decades later, **he flinches at closeness like it's a trap**.

So, while you're over there thinking, *"Why won't he come closer?"*, he's quietly panicking: *"If I let her in, I'll lose myself."*

His withdrawal isn't always cruelty. Sometimes it's conditioning. Sometimes it's trauma. Sometimes it's just the result of being a little boy who was told to **man up, shut down, and never need anyone**. And now, here you are — needing him. Emotionally. Deeply. Clearly. And that terrifies him.

No one ever taught him how to show up without shutting down.

And no, this is not an excuse. It's an explanation. **You can have empathy for his wiring without making it your problem to fix**.

But understanding this is the first step to stepping out of the blame-shame spiral. You're not "too much." And he's not necessarily evil. You're just speaking love in two different dialects — one is cling, one is ghost.

And when those two attachment styles collide?

One of you keeps proving your love by overgiving. The other keeps proving their independence by under-responding.

That doesn't mean it's doomed. But it sure as hell means it's going to take work. Real work. From **both** of you.

He has to learn that intimacy doesn't mean engulfment. You have to learn that distance doesn't always mean abandonment. And both of you have to meet in the messy middle — where regulation, communication, and **mutual effort** live.

But here's what I need you to hear loud and clear:

His fear of closeness isn't more important than your need for it.

You shouldn't have to shrink, silence, or self-soothe just to keep him from feeling overwhelmed. If he wants a relationship, he needs to learn how to **be in one**.

And if he's unwilling to look at his wiring?

Then all the empathy in the world won't keep the rubber band from snapping.

He Wasn't Taught to Show Up, He Was Taught to Shut Down

The Emotional Disempowerment of Modern Men

You want to know the punchline? **He was never given a chance either.**

No, this isn't an excuse. But it **is** part of the story. Because while you were being taught to accommodate, anticipate, and endlessly give… he was being told to toughen up, shut it down, and never show weakness. That stuff didn't disappear, it just got rebranded.

And so, in 2025, what we're left with is a whole generation of men who were robbed of their emotional muscles and then dropped into relationships where emotional labor is **the** currency. They're emotionally illiterate, then punished for not speaking the language.

That's not your fault, but it is your reality.

Because patriarchy didn't just screw women by handing us the never-ending to-do list, it screwed men by stealing their emotional toolkit. They were told "man up" instead of "let it out." They were taught that vulnerability = weakness, asking for help = failure, and introspection = indulgence. Add to that the rising social backlash of "get it right or get cancelled," and now they're terrified of saying the wrong thing **and** incapable of saying the right one.

So, what do they do instead? They hide. They deflect. They play dumb. They ghost. They opt out of hard conversations. They outsource the emotional labor to you, the woman who seems to have it all together.

And **sometimes we let them**, because it feels easier to do it ourselves than to sit through the slow, painful process of watching them fumble through emotional kindergarten.

But we pay the price. Every time.

It's not just the "man-child" trope anymore, it's emotional underdevelopment wrapped in charisma, hidden behind ambition, or disguised as introversion. It's men who **want** connection but were never taught how to build it. Who crave intimacy but collapse under the weight of accountability. Who say, *"I'm just not good at feelings"* and expect that to be enough.

Breaking news: **it's not enough**.

And no, you can't teach him. You can't therapize him into adulthood. You can't rewrite 30+ years of social conditioning with one good heart and a list of communication strategies. You are not the antidote to his emotional neglect.

He has to want it. He has to choose growth. He has to look in the mirror and say, *"I wasn't given the tools, but it's about time I build them now."*

Until then, you're not "too emotional." You're not "too much." You're just standing in front of a man still running outdated software, hoping he'll install the update without throwing the whole system into a shutdown.

Let this land: **empathy does not require enmeshment**.

You can feel for him and still expect more.

You can understand the why and still set the what-the-hell boundary.

You can love him and still walk away if he refuses to rise.

Modern masculinity is confused. And that's not on you to fix. But it **is** your responsibility to decide whether you want to build a life around someone who still thinks "emotional maturity" is optional.

Because if he can learn how to fix a car, run a business, game for eight hours straight, or memorize every Marvel backstory… he can learn how to communicate, regulate, and show the hell up.

If he wants to.

Why Emotional Maturity Wasn't Modeled, Expected, or Rewarded

Most men weren't raised to be emotionally mature because **no one around them was modeling it, expecting it, or giving a damn gold star for it.**

You can't become fluent in a language no one speaks around you. And you sure as hell don't practice it if every time you try, you're mocked, shut down, or told to "man up."

Here's the thing that gets missed in the gender wars: **little boys get emotionally stunted, not because they're broken, but because we break them early.** Don't get me started on what really happens when you raise boys on a steady diet of "don't cry," "suck it up," and "be a man."

You don't just raise someone who doesn't express emotion, you raise someone who doesn't know how to **connect**. Not to himself and not to others. Not even to the woman he loves most in the world. And now **we** reap this grim harvest.

Because when you're taught that vulnerability is weakness, you armor up. And when you armor up, you stay distant — even in bed, even in marriage, even when your whole damn life depends on building closeness.

"Boys don't cry" sounds innocent until you realize it's f*king emotional amputation. You don't just lose the tears, you lose the wiring that tells you how to say, *"I miss you,"* or *"I'm scared,"* or *"That hurt."* Instead, you get silence. You get detachment. You get men who blow up when they feel vulnerable, and shut down when you need them most.

Connection isn't just cuddling on the couch or tagging you in memes. It's honesty. It's presence. It's the ability to sit in emotional discomfort without rage-quitting the moment you get real.

And while girls were handed the emotional mop and told to clean up everyone's messes with empathy and grace, boys were handed a stick and told to fight their way through discomfort.

The result? A grown man who feels deep love for you but cannot, for the life of him, express it without fumbling like a 14-year-old in a middle school hallway. A man who knows you're hurting but doesn't know how to respond without either fixing, fleeing, or shutting down.

Why? Because emotions were never modeled. Not by their dads. Not by their coaches. Not by the movies they watched or the friends they grew up with. Emotional vulnerability was either ridiculed or punished. And the rare time it **was** expressed, it usually came out in anger, because **that** was the only emotion deemed masculine enough to be acceptable.

So, what happens when they hit adulthood and suddenly find themselves in relationships where emotional literacy is the price of admission?

They panic. They either go full caveman (*"What? I said I love you that one time in 2014!"*) or freeze like a deer in headlights the moment you bring up feelings.

Now here's where it gets even more twisted: **Not only was emotional maturity never modeled, it was actively discouraged.**

Men who show softness are seen as weak. Men who seek help are seen as broken. Men who set emotional boundaries or express their inner world are often told they're being dramatic or needy

Meanwhile, emotional intelligence? Labeled "too sensitive" or "soft." So, tell me — **why would he evolve if the world gave him a standing ovation for staying stunted?**

"Boys don't cry" wasn't just a bad slogan. **It became a generational trauma.** And unless he's willing to break that chain, you'll always feel like you're in a relationship with half a person.

And let's not forget the reward system. Emotional restraint? Applauded. Even considered sexy (hello, Marlon Brando, James Dean and Sean Connery!). Stoicism? Admired. Blow-ups followed by silent sulking? Chalked up to "just how he is."

This isn't about letting him off the hook. This is about naming the reality: he wasn't raised with emotional maturity as a goal, so it's no wonder he never chased it.

But here's the catch — **you were.**

You were raised to notice how everyone felt, adjust your tone, cushion your truths, and carry the weight of unspoken tensions. So, it feels **normal** to overfunction emotionally. To do the work for two. To give him credit for trying while silently bleeding out from unmet needs. This is what they called being a "good woman".

Let me be blunt: it's not your job to lower the standard just because he grew up like this.

You didn't create the wound, but you don't need to bleed for it either.

The world failed him? That sucks.

He wants to stay emotionally stagnant because it's easier? That's his choice.

You choosing peace, maturity, and mutuality? That's yours.

How Society Screwed You Both (and How You Reclaim Yourselves)

The Feminist Win That Turned Into a Burnout Sentence

There's a Ukrainian saying that goes something like this: *"Make a fool bow to God and he'll break his forehead."* In other words, give a human a good idea, just one sacred truth, and watch us butcher it into something unrecognizable, exaggerated, and borderline absurd. We've done it with religion, with tolerance, and yep… with feminism too.

Because somewhere between "equal rights" and "girlboss until you bleed," the feminist win turned into a silent burnout sentence.

It started with power. Freedom. The right to say "no," to choose, to vote, to work, to walk away. But then came the silent shift. Suddenly you weren't just free to do it all, you were **expected** to. Full-time job, full-time mom, full-time emotional pack mule for a man who still thinks he's "not good at feelings."

We raised the bar for ourselves and called it progress. But no one told the men to meet us there.

And now here you are: exhausted, overfunctioning, eating dinner over the sink, and wondering why being empowered feels a lot like being emotionally exiled.

Feminism didn't fail you. But the culture around it sure as hell contorted it.

You were promised liberation and got overextension. You were told you didn't need anyone, and internalized that as "you shouldn't ask for help." You learned to pay your bills, carry your partner's emotional baggage, and never, ever drop the ball. And if you did? You'd better not cry about it, because **strong women don't complain**, they power through.

Bullshit.

Let's stop calling that progress.

Let's start calling it what it is: a cultural bait-and-switch that needs a serious rewrite.

The Masculinity Crisis That Nobody Wants to Talk About

Let's just admit it: **we're in the middle of a full-blown masculinity identity crisis**, and no one knows what the hell to do with it. Not the men, not the women, not the therapists, not the podcasts, and definitely not the influencers screaming "Real men cry!" one minute and "Step up, king!" the next.

It's chaotic. It's confusing. And it's leaving a whole generation of men emotionally stuck, somewhere between caveman and sentient houseplant.

For decades, men were told to man up. Don't cry. Provide. Protect. Be strong. Never crack. Never feel. And while those old-school rules were suffocating, they were at least **clear**. You knew the game, even if it was rigged.

Then came the shift. Emotional intelligence became sexy. Toxic masculinity got called out (as it should), but in the process, a lot of men were left without a map. They were told **what not to be**, but not **what to become instead**.

So now they're floating. Frozen. Afraid to be too soft, afraid to be too assertive, and mostly just... afraid. Of women. Of failing. Of being called out. Of saying the wrong thing. Of getting it wrong. Of not knowing how to fix what they were never taught to feel.

And if we're being honest? Some of them just opted out. Checked out emotionally. Stuck their fingers in their ears and went, *"La-la-la, let me watch Joe Rogan and lift weights until this all blows over."*

You can't heal what you won't name. And our culture still doesn't want to name what's really going on, that masculinity itself is in a no man's land, caught between "be better" and "don't exist."

And guess who's stuck holding the relational consequences? You. The woman in the partnership. The one who's told to "just communicate better" when he shuts down, explodes, or clams up like a terrified little boy hiding behind bravado.

It's not about hating men. It's about noticing what's happening to them, and how **we're the ones carrying the fallout.**

You didn't cause this. But you're sure as hell paying for it.

And until more men are willing to get uncomfortable — really uncomfortable — we're just going to keep dancing this same sad tango, where women evolve and men... endure.

Let's talk about why that dance ends with you carrying both people across the floor.

The Path Back to Emotional Equity

Emotional equity isn't found in viral quotes, or in well-meaning slogans about "letting men feel." It's not going to be handed to us by a culture that still can't decide whether sensitivity is strength or weakness, or whether women should be CEOs or emotional sponges, or both while smiling.

We're not walking back to balance by swinging the pendulum in the opposite direction, either. You don't fix inequity by becoming the oppressor in heels, or by watering down masculinity until it's just passivity in a hoodie. We've already tried obedience. We've tried martyrdom. We've tried yelling. And still, somehow, we're exhausted.

The only way forward is through truth. Messy, uncomfortable, burn-your-ego truth.

The kind of truth that says: *"I've been overfunctioning because I thought that's what love looked like."*

Or: *"I shut down because no one ever taught me how to be vulnerable without being punished for it."*

Or: *"We're not enemies, but we are unequally armed."*

This is where we stop playing roles. Where we stop turning "masculinity" into a trauma response and "femininity" into a prison of self-sacrifice. Where we stop blaming each other and start holding mirrors to our own behaviors, without shame, but with accountability.

We don't need more real men or strong women. We need **whole people**, who can sit in the discomfort of growth without making it everyone else's problem. People who can say *"I hurt you"* without collapsing and hear *"I need more"* without deflecting. People who don't just stay, they **show up**.

Because emotional equity doesn't come from silence or screaming. It comes from seeing each other fully and still choosing to do the work.

And if your partner can meet you there — honestly, fully, with humility and effort — then you're not just lucky, you're aligned.

But if he can't, or won't, or chooses comfort over growth again and again, then at least now you'll see it clearly. And you'll know what to do next.

You won't be guessing. You won't be waiting. You won't be shrinking.

You'll be moving forward with your eyes wide open, and your self-worth intact.

Now let's wrap this up.

CHAPTER 11:

REDEFINING LOVE
(SO YOU DON'T REPEAT THE PATTERN)

Rewrite the Fairy Tale

Trade Chaos for Calm: Rewrite What "Happily Ever After" Actually Means

Once upon a time, "happily ever after" meant a man with good shoulders, a dark past, and **just enough emotional damage to keep things interesting**. You know the type — moodier than a monsoon season, but oh-so-charming in the apology phase. We were trained that love was supposed to feel like **work**, as long as you loved hard enough, cried dramatically enough, and stuck around long enough to inspire his personal transformation montage.

And if it didn't hurt a little?

Well, maybe you weren't doing it right.

That kind of story rewired your brain to **confuse chaos with chemistry** and made you believe that love wasn't real unless you were lowkey exhausted all the time. And I know this, because I was in one of those "forever" relationships — the kind where you're so deep in the dysfunction that even your therapist needs a therapist.

He was intense. "Sensitive." He made me responsible for every single one of his feelings. If he was spiraling, it was because I'd disappointed him. If he shut down, I should've phrased things better. I became the emotional tech support line for his entire inner world. I apologized constantly. I agreed to things I didn't want to do, just to keep the peace. And I convinced myself that if I could just keep him calm, I'd finally earn rest (yeah, keep dreaming babe).

At some point, I stopped making decisions. I stopped having opinions. I stopped recognizing myself.

And then I broke — like, actual breakdown broke.

The kind where you're on the floor, not metaphorically, but literally, gasping for air, wanting to rip out that anvil out of your chest... wondering how the hell I became the side character in my own life.

When I finally found the strength to end it, I still couldn't say, *"You're not for me."* I said, *"I'm not for you,"* because I had been so conditioned to protect his feelings, and I was terrified of the emotional backlash I knew would follow. And sure enough, it came. The moment he realized I was serious, he started threatening to kill himself.

And leaving? It didn't feel triumphant.

It felt like someone unplugged me from my own life. I wasn't happy. I wasn't relieved. I was numb.

I was so used to being overstimulated by emotional chaos that peace felt like a coma.

But eventually, I started to remember myself. I started laughing again - real laughter, not the kind you do to de-escalate a grown man's temper tantrum. And I realized, **this** is what real love is supposed to feel like.

It's not **fireworks**. It's **not** dramatic highs and unbearable lows. It's not passion laced with panic.

It's waking up and not checking your tone before you say good morning.

It's resting without guilt and being able to laugh at something dumb without wondering if he's going to ruin the mood over dinner.

It's boring. Beautifully, gloriously boring. Free.

So yeah, "happily ever after" doesn't look like what we were sold.

It looks like:

- A soft Sunday with no tension in the air

- A partner who doesn't require twelve disclaimers before a conversation

- A home that feels like peace, not emotional cleanup on aisle five

- Loving someone who doesn't need a growth curriculum and a warning label

---

Your Calm-AF "Happily Ever After" Checklist

- ✓ You don't need to overthink your tone before asking for something

- ✓ You feel safe being vulnerable and aren't punished for having needs

- ✓ You're not confused or walking on eggshells

- ✓ You don't have to emotionally parent someone to feel secure

- ✓ You can rest, and I mean actual, nervous-system-downregulated rest

- ✓ You like who you are **in** the relationship (and not just when you're alone)

So, forget the brooding bad boy. Forget the one you had to fix before he could love you back. And forget any story that told you love had to hurt to count. And write your new fairy tale.

Make it peaceful. Make it quiet. Make it boring as hell in the best possible way.

Because one day, someone's going to walk into your life and you're not going to have to fight, beg, or fix a damn thing. I know.

And it's going to feel so different, you'll almost miss the chaos.

Almost.

And if you're wondering whether peaceful love can still knock the breath out of you, whether it can still be electric without being traumatic, I'll tell you what I know:

He's the kind of man who doesn't walk into a room to dominate it, but somehow, everyone feels his presence, and no one dares cross him. He carries that kind of quiet, grounded power that doesn't need performance. And with me? He's never once made me feel small. Not once. Not for my emotions, my intensity, my ambition, my softness, none of it. He tells me I'm a queen. A goddess. And it never feels like flattery, it feels like he's just speaking the truth he sees every day.

Yes, our life isn't smooth. There's chaos everywhere around us. External storms trying to tear everything apart. But when we're together, it's like being in the eye of it. Total stillness. Total clarity. It reminds me of that scene in *The Witcher* — remember the one where Pavetta's powers exploded into a full-blown storm that nearly destroyed the entire castle, but in the center of it, she and her lover were just… still. Connected. Oblivious to everything but each other.

And I know, with every part of me, that **this** is what love should feel like. Not constant turmoil. Not emotional sacrifice. Not fear dressed up as passion. But two people standing in the storm, untouched by it, because they're finally, completely, home.

Peaceful Doesn't Mean Boring — How to Tell the Difference

If you've spent years in emotionally unpredictable relationships like I did, then calm might feel suspicious. Peaceful might register as flat. Even kindness might weirdly feel... dull. And that's not because you're shallow, it's because your nervous system has been trained to equate chaos with connection.

When you're used to walking on eggshells, tension becomes your baseline. So, when that tension disappears, it doesn't always feel like relief. It feels like something's missing. You might catch yourself thinking, *"Shouldn't this feel more exciting? Where's the spark?"* But here's the hard truth: if your "spark" was built on anxiety, adrenaline, or the thrill of emotional whiplash, it wasn't a spark. It was a survival response.

So how do you tell the difference between **boring** and **peaceful**?

Peaceful Love Feels Like This:

- You're not constantly wondering where you stand.

- You're not decoding texts or tone shifts.

- You feel **safe**, not sleepy.

- You can relax, not numb out.

- You laugh more. You think clearer. Your body isn't bracing 24/7.

- You like who you are in the relationship, because you're not constantly shape-shifting.

What "Boring" Love (That's Actually Just Emotionally Regulated) Is NOT:

- Emotionally flat.

- Sexless or disconnected (believe you me!)

- Lacking chemistry.

- Passive or uninspiring.

- Code for "I'm settling."

It's actually the kind of connection where you stop spending all your energy scanning for danger and start spending it on being present.

But that can feel disorienting at first. You might even self-sabotage. You might pick fights just to feel something. You might test them just to make sure they **really** care. That's your trauma talking, not your intuition.

So how do you know if it's safe or stale?

Ask Yourself:

- Do I feel like I can be myself without performance?

- Am I relaxed when we're together, or just... detached?

- Does this feel emotionally steady *or* emotionally dead?

- Do I feel **more me** around him or less?

Bottom line: Peace is not the absence of passion. It's the foundation for it.

And if you're bored, check your patterns before you check out. The most dangerous thing isn't that you'll end up in a "boring" relationship. It's that you'll leave a safe one chasing the high of dysfunction you've been trained to confuse with love.

And you're too damn wise now to fall for that again.

Nervous System Cues: What Your Body's Telling You Before Your Brain Catches Up

You know that feeling in your gut when something's off, but you can't quite explain why? That subtle tension in your shoulders, the way your chest tightens when he enters the room, or how you suddenly start talking softer, slower, less like **you**?

That's your nervous system trying to save your ass before your brain spins up another round of excuses.

Your body always knows before your logic does.

Especially if you've been in high-stress or emotionally imbalanced relationships, your nervous system becomes your early warning system. But the problem is, if you've spent years overriding it, telling yourself *"I'm just being sensitive"* or *"he didn't mean it like that"*, you might not know how to trust those signals anymore.

Let's change that.

Here's what to watch for:

When You're NOT Safe (Even if He's Smiling):

- You feel a rush of adrenaline when he texts, **but not the good kind**.

- Your stomach drops when he says, *"we need to talk."*

- You find yourself preparing, rehearsing, or softening your words out of fear.

- Your body tenses when you're around him, even when nothing "bad" is happening.

- You're constantly scanning his mood before you speak or move.

- You feel tired after every interaction, not nourished.

That's not love. That's your nervous system doing full-time crisis management.

What Safety Feels Like Instead:

- You breathe deeper around him without even realizing it.

- Your shoulders drop. Your jaw unclenches. Your voice stays steady.

- You say what you need and you don't immediately regret it.

- You don't have to explain your silence, your moods, or your history in a tone so careful it might as well be PR.

- You feel steady, not hyperalert. Connected, not drained.

Your nervous system isn't just some abstract wellness concept, it's a literal signal that tells you if your environment (or your partner) is **safe or dangerous.**

And if your body is constantly on edge around someone?

It's not because you're damaged. It's because **your body is brilliant**.

So, here's what to do next time you're unsure about someone:

Quick Gut Check Exercise:

1. Close your eyes.

2. Picture yourself sitting next to him in silence. No conversation. No distractions.

3. Now ask:

    o   Is my body soft or tense?

    o   Do I feel calm or like I'm prepping for something?

    o   Do I want to move closer or lean away?

Don't analyze it. Don't explain it. Just **notice**.

Your body has always known what your brain was too polite to say out loud.

So, listen.

Because she — the version of you who had to keep her guard up just to survive a relationship?

She's exhausted. And she deserves a relationship where she doesn't have to be on high alert just to be loved.

Green Flags & Grown Standards

What Emotional Maturity Actually Looks Like

Forget charm. Forget chemistry. Forget if he owns a copy of *The Four Agreements* and lights incense. None of that matters if he can't handle his own emotions without melting down, lashing out, or disappearing into his man cave for 48 hours every time you express a feeling.

You want to know if someone's emotionally mature? Don't ask what he **says**. Watch what he **does when things get uncomfortable**.

Here's what you're looking for, not perfection, but **emotional adulthood**:

Grown-Man Green Flags:

- He owns his impact, even when it wasn't intentional.

- He can hear feedback without crumbling, attacking, or deflecting.

- He doesn't need you to pad every sentence with disclaimers just to get through to him.

- He doesn't treat your needs like a personal insult.

- He doesn't weaponize his past as a reason to act like an ass.

- He knows when to talk, and when to take a damn breath.

If You're Still Not Sure, Ask:

- Can he name what he's feeling without turning it into a monologue about **how hard things are for him right now?**

- Can he hold space for **your** emotions without trying to fix, explain, or turn it into a therapy session about his ex?

- Can he apologize without a thesis statement and a guilt trip?

- Can he disagree with you without making it a power struggle?

If the answer to most of these is **yes**, you're not dealing with a unicorn, you're dealing with someone who has done the inner work. And that's rarer than you think.

Reminder:

Emotional maturity isn't about being "nice." It's about being **steady, self-aware, and accountable**. It's someone who shows up consistently, communicates clearly, and doesn't need you to mother, manage, or motivate them into being decent.

So no, you're not asking for too much.

You're asking for someone who can sit at the emotional adult table and eat with a knife and fork.

Anything less?

You're just parenting in lipstick again.

Personal Story: The "Therapist Girlfriend" Trap

I used to think I was just emotionally intelligent. Empathetic. Good at relationships. The kind of woman who could de-escalate anything with enough grace and strategic breathing.

Mhm… I was not being emotionally intelligent. I was being emotionally overextended. I wasn't a partner, I was a **f*cking support team**. A one-woman call center for his nervous system. Emotional tech support, open 24/7.

If he was spiraling, I dropped everything to talk him down. If he shut down, I waited in silence, soothed his ego, and blamed myself for "pushing too hard." If he lashed out, I wondered where exactly I had gone wrong. I used to rewrite texts five times just to make sure I didn't "trigger" him.

He didn't have to regulate anything, because I did it for him.

And I didn't call it caretaking. I called it **love**.

I thought I was just being understanding. Patient. Compassionate.

What I was really being… was **f*cking exhausted**.

And no one saw it. Not even me. Because I was still functioning. Still smiling. Still playing the role of "the strong one." Meanwhile, every interaction was draining me like a leaky faucet I didn't know how to fix.

He got to fall apart whenever he wanted.

I had to stay grounded, gentle, emotionally literate and **apologetic**.

That was the part that broke me. Not the tantrums, not the mood swings, not the sulking. The way I started saying sorry for things I didn't even do, just to keep the temperature down.

Because if I didn't manage his emotions, who would?

If I didn't buffer his triggers, what would happen?

If I stopped fixing… would everything fall apart?

That's when I realized — **if your relationship only works when you're functioning like a therapist with benefits**, it's not a relationship. It's emotional codependency dressed up as maturity.

I wasn't emotionally wise. I was emotionally manipulated.

And once I stopped performing emotional CPR every time he panicked, the whole thing collapsed, because that was the glue holding it together: **me, overfunctioning**.

Communication, Self-Regulation, Consistency: The Holy Trinity

You want to know if a man is ready for real partnership? Don't look at his job. Don't look at his hobbies. Don't even look at how well he treats a waiter. Look at **these three things,** because they are the backbone of every emotionally healthy relationship:

Communication. Self-Regulation. Consistency.

If one of these is missing, it's only a matter of time before you're doing the emotional labor for two again.

Let's break them down:

1. Communication: Can He Talk Without Blaming or Hiding?

- Can he say how he feels without putting it all on you?

- Can he handle direct conversation without turning it into a court-room scene?

- Does he actually **listen**, or just wait for his turn to talk?

- Does he avoid hard conversations or face them calmly and directly?

Healthy communication isn't about having deep heart-to-hearts every night. It's about being able to speak the truth without dancing around it or ducking behind ego. If you're constantly guessing what he means or decoding emotional Morse code, that's not mystery, it's **emotional immaturity.**

2. Self-Regulation: Can He Handle Discomfort Without Exploding or Ghosting?

- Can he stay present when he's upset or does he vanish, shut down, or lash out?

- Does he take a breath or go straight to blame?

- When he's triggered, can he own it without dragging you into the fire?

Self-regulation means **he doesn't outsource his emotional mess to you**. You're not walking on eggshells. You're not tiptoeing around his moods. You're not apologizing for needing anything because it might set him off.

3. Consistency: Does He Show Up Like He Means It — Every Time?

- Do his actions match his words?

- Does he show up on the good days **and** the hard ones?

- Is he the same person on Wednesday that he was on Saturday?

Consistency isn't sexy, but it's sacred. It's what builds trust. It's what allows you to **relax**. And if you're feeling anxious more often than not, chances are you're dealing with inconsistency, and your body knows it.

Final Gut Check:

- Do I feel emotionally safe with him or emotionally hungry?

- Do I trust what he says or do I keep hoping it'll finally match what he does?

- Do I feel like I'm in a partnership or in a PR campaign where I'm the only one showing up?

When all three of these are present, you'll feel it. Not in fireworks, but in your **nervous system finally relaxing**. In the way your voice steadies. In the ease of being able to just… exist.

That's the standard now.

No more explaining emotional basics to grown men.

If he doesn't speak the language of truth, regulation, and follow-through, he's not fluent enough to date you.

I saw it. Once I stepped back, I saw who he **chose** to be without my cushioning. And that told me more than a thousand heart-to-hearts ever could.

Build-Your-Own "I Will Not Settle for Less Than This" Checklist

Now that you've burned the blueprint of emotional chaos, it's time to write your own manual.

Not for anyone else in the world, for *you*.

So that when someone walks into your life, you're not squinting at red flags or doing mental gymnastics to justify crumbs. You're crystal clear on what you stand for, and what you're **done** settling for.

This isn't your Pinterest dream board. This is your **minimum standard list**. Your **emotional contract with yourself**. Your **hell yes or hell no** criteria.

How to Build It:

Grab a notebook, your Notes app, a napkin, whatever. And write:

"I will not settle for a relationship that requires me to…"

Then finish that sentence. As many times as you need. Like:

- …apologize for having needs

- …be the only one doing emotional labor

- …explain basic respect

- …tiptoe around someone's triggers

- …coach a grown man through communication 101

- …shrink myself to be palatable

- …guess where I stand

- …beg for clarity

- …confuse drama with passion

- …earn love through suffering

Now flip it. Write:

"I will only invest in a relationship where…"

- …my boundaries are respected without debate

- …I feel safe being fully seen and fully expressed

- …conflict isn't a crisis, it's a conversation

- …consistency is the default, not the reward

- …I am celebrated, not just tolerated

- …there is space for joy, rest, and mutual growth

Non-Negotiables Are Not "High Standards"

Stop calling yourself picky. You're **discerning**.

Stop worrying you'll scare someone off. If your standards scare them, *good*, they just saved you time.

Your checklist isn't a wall. It's a **filter.**

It keeps out what exhausts you and protects what you've fought so hard to rebuild.

And if you meet someone who makes you start justifying scraps again?

Pull this list out. Read it out loud.

And remind yourself: **I didn't survive all that to end up back in the same story with a different face.**

Staying Open Without Losing Yourself

How to Date Again Without Walking Into the Same Trap

You've done the work. You've burned the old rulebook. You're no longer trying to be chosen, you're choosing. But now what?

Now you re-enter the world not as someone hoping to be loved, but as someone who **knows exactly what she's not doing again.**

You are not:

- Dating potential.

- Mislabeling chaos as chemistry.

- Downplaying red flags because he's "nice" or "hot" or "trauma-bond compatible."

No. You are dating with **clarity** now.

But here's the thing: clarity doesn't mean coldness.

You don't need to build a fortress around your heart, you just need to **stay awake.**

Start with These Rules of Engagement:

1. Don't rush to define it, watch it.

Let the first few weeks be about observation, not projection.

You're not interviewing for "boyfriend." You're gathering data. How does he handle awkward moments? Minor disappointment? A boundary?

2. Listen to what your body says, not just what he says.

If you're anxious after every date and calling it butterflies? That's not excitement. That's your nervous system throwing red flags like it's working overtime. Peace should not feel like boredom. Presence should not feel like a test.

3. Don't override yellow flags just because there are no red ones.

If he never asks about you, if you feel drained after every conversation, **if something just feels off — pause.** You don't need a dramatic exit. Just don't keep feeding energy into something that's already poking holes in your peace.

What You're Looking For Now:

- Does he follow up when he says he will?

- Does he ask thoughtful questions or just talk about himself for 90 minutes straight?

- Can you be honest without prepping for his emotional collapse?

- Do you feel more like yourself with him or less?

That's the checklist now. Not just *"Do I like him?"* but ***"Do I like who I am when I'm with him?"***

You don't need to date like you've got something to prove. You're not broken. You're not behind. You're not trying to make up for lost time.

You're just here to connect with someone who brings peace, not performance.

If it's not aligned, let it go. You've already survived the storm.

You don't need to audition for the next one.

Spot Early Manipulation, Love Bombing, or Conflict Avoidance

You don't need to become a suspicious robot scanning every man for defects, but you **do** need to know what early manipulation looks like before it dresses itself up as "intimacy." Because the truth is, a lot of dysfunction doesn't show up on date one with a pitchfork. It shows up with charm. Attunement. Intensity. And a playlist you weirdly also love.

So, here's the golden rule: **if it feels too good to be true too fast, pause.**

You've done this before, and now you know how to spot the difference between connection and coercion.

What Early Manipulation Might Look Like:

- He mirrors your personality perfectly and says *"I've never felt this way before"*... by week two.

- He says all the right things, but they feel rehearsed, like he's **auditioning for intimacy**, not building it.

- He calls you "his person," "his queen," "the one" before he even knows your middle name.

- You feel like you **should** be excited, but you're already on edge.

That's not fate. That's love bombing.

And the danger? It works because it feels like a shortcut to the connection you've always craved. But it's not real closeness. It's control with flowers.

What Conflict Avoidance Might Look Like:

- He never gets upset, but you feel like you're the only one being honest.

- Every disagreement ends with *"It's fine,"* *"Whatever,"* or a hard subject change.

- He shuts down or disappears instead of engaging when something gets real.

- He insists on "keeping the vibe good" when you're trying to talk about something that matters.

That's not emotional maturity. That's **emotional evasion.**

People who can't engage in conflict can't build intimacy.

If you can't bring up something uncomfortable without him ghosting, stonewalling, or giving you the "you're too much" look? That's not a vibe protector. That's an emotional escape artist.

Your Clarity Filters:

Ask yourself:

- Is this moving faster than my body feels safe with?

- Am I saying yes because I'm excited or because I feel flattered, overwhelmed, or pressured?

- Is he open to the messy, awkward, unfiltered parts of me or just obsessed with the polished version?

And remember: **consistency over intensity. Always.**

It's easy to create a fantasy connection in two weeks.

It takes **real emotional stamina** to show up steadily for someone in a way that's sustainable.

So, stay awake. Stay open. And when your gut says, *"Slow down"* — **listen**.

The goal isn't to be paranoid. It's to be **proactive**.

Boundaries in Action: Holding Your Center Without Hardening Your Heart

Here's what no one tells you when you finally get your peace back: it's tempting to build a fortress around it. After what you've been through, "never again" turns into "no one gets close." And honestly? That makes sense. But the goal isn't to become untouchable, it's to become unshakeable.

You don't need walls.

You need **boundaries that move with you.**

Boundaries that protect, not isolate, clarify, not punish. That allow love in, but only when it respects the rules of your emotional house.

How to Set a Boundary (Without Feeling Like a Monster):

1. **Get clear on the rule, before the conflict.** You don't wait for the moment he crosses the line to decide what your limit is. You already know: *If I'm dismissed, I speak up. If I'm not heard, I don't keep explaining. If I'm disrespected, I walk.*

2. **Say it early. Say it calmly. Say it without a damn Power-Point.**

3. **Boundaries don't require justification.** They don't need a backstory. They sound like:

   o   *"That doesn't work for me."*

   o   *"I'm not okay with that."*

   o   *"If this continues, I'll need to step back."*

4. **Don't wait for him to agree. Respect is not a group decision.** Your boundary isn't a request, it's a standard. If someone pushes against it? That's the data you need. You're not being "harsh", you're observing behavior and responding accordingly.

The Heart of It: Soft Doesn't Mean Collapsible

You can stay open. Loving. Warm. Curious.

But you do it from a place of grounded truth.

You don't bend every time someone seems "nice."

You don't backtrack just because they're sad.

You don't drop your standard because they "didn't mean it."

You hold your center, keep your softness.

You let people earn closeness, not just waltz into it because they said the right thing on date three.

Boundaries are not about keeping people out. They're about **keeping you in**. Fully. Freely. Safely.

Because now that you've come home to yourself, the only people allowed in the door are the ones who **knock respectfully, and wipe their feet.**

Cautionary Tale of Dave.

From me to you.

To show you that red flags like that don't just show up in brooding bad boys or emotionally stunted Peter Pans. Sometimes, it comes dressed in charisma, intelligence, and just the right amount of faux vulnerability to make you second-guess your gut.

Dave was Harvard-polished and fluent in Brené/Gottman. He didn't yell, he "processed." He ran the relationship like a coaching program where I was the client. With literal spreadsheets (yup, mapping out needs/wants/likes and deconstructing every bloody fiber of my being).

If my energy dipped, he withdrew into tragic silence until I performed emotional CPR. On paper it looked like accountability; in my body it felt like guilt in leadership language.

When war broke out in Ukraine and my family was still there, I was barely functioning. One night, because I couldn't be bright and attuned on command, he collapsed into a pout and made my grief about his "trust issues."

Another time, I was at the nail salon with foil on my fingers, unable to text. He spiraled. Later, when I explained, he narrowed his eyes and said: *"Oh. So that was more important than me?"*

That was the click: it didn't matter how "evolved" and self-aware he sounded, how beautifully he named his triggers, or how many personal development frameworks he flaunted. When my joy dimmed or I needed care, he crumbled and made me responsible for fixing it.

Bottom line: Weaponized vulnerability is still control, it just wears a softer voice. Emotional fluency without self-regulation is performance, not partnership.

Stay soft, stay open, but never at the cost of disappearing to keep someone else intact.

The Vow

Read this out loud. Today. Then again whenever you need it.

- I trade chaos for clarity.

- I will not earn love by abandoning myself.

- My body's cues outrank anyone's charm.

- I choose partners fluent in truth, regulation, and consistency.

- If peace feels "boring," I breathe until my nervous system remembers.

- My boundaries are house rules, not warnings.

- I bless what was, release what isn't, and protect what is mine: my peace.

Place your hand on your chest. Inhale 4, hold 4, exhale 6.
Say: ***"No more."***
Then: ***"Now me."***

From → To (the whole book in eight lines)

- From fixing → to witnessing.

- From potential → to proof.

- From intensity → to consistency.

- From decoding → to directness.

- From apology → to boundary.

- From auditioning → to choosing.

- From hunger → to enough.

- From overfunctioning → to being held.

Your Next Three Moves

1. Set your **"I Will Not Settle…"** list as your phone lock screen for 30 days.

2. Before any reply you might regret, do **4–4–6 breathing** and say: *"This is a trigger, not a sign. I choose peace."*

3. Share your vow with one trusted friend and ask for **honest mirroring** if you start calling anxiety "chemistry."

This isn't the beginning of another performance. It's the end of over-functioning, and the start of a life that never asks you to disappear to be loved.

273

CONCLUSION:

THIS ISN'T ABOUT HIM, IT'S ABOUT YOU FINALLY COMING HOME TO YOURSELF

This was never a breakup manual, never a war cry against men, and definitely not a polished self-help pep talk tied with a bow.

It was a reckoning.

A reckoning with the version of you who kept trying harder when it hurt. With the fantasy you fed because reality was too painful to name. With the quiet exhaustion of overfunctioning in relationships that demanded your soul but couldn't hold your truth.

This book was about finally seeing the cost of doing everyone else's emotional labor — and calling it love.

Maybe it started small, with soft-spoken betrayals you didn't even recognize as betrayals: skipping your needs, managing his moods, apologizing for your tone even when your words were clean. Then one day, something cracked, and you couldn't unsee it. The imbalance. The burnout. The knowing.

That's what this was always about.

Not leaving or staying.

Not labeling him toxic.

Not waiting for a cinematic finale.

Just seeing it. Naming it. Owning your part in the overgiving, and deciding… at last — to choose yourself.

Maybe you stayed and tried one last time, without the clipboard, without the coaching, without the emotional CPR. Maybe you stepped back and let him show you who he was without your scaffolding. And maybe he rose to it.

Or maybe he didn't.

Maybe the story ended not with a bang, but with the soft, exhausted closing of a door you finally realized was never yours to keep propping open.

And maybe it broke your heart, but also gave it back to you.

Either way, you stopped chasing potential and started listening to your body. You stopped calling anxiety chemistry. You stopped mistaking pain for proof. You finally stopped auditioning for love like it was a role someone else had to cast you in.

Here's what I hope you carry from these pages:

- **Your peace is not optional. It's the baseline.**

- **Your needs are not too much. They're the map.**

- **You can miss someone and still never go back.**

- **You can crave love and still walk away from anything that confuses addiction with intimacy.**

- **You're not a fixer, a therapist, or a motivational speaker with good eyebrows and a nervous system on fire.**

- **You're a woman with one wild, irreplaceable life.**

You didn't "end up" in the wrong story. You simply woke up mid-scene, realized the script wasn't yours, and walked yourself off that stage.

So, whether you're rebuilding love with someone new or rewriting it where you stand, don't lead with caretaking. Lead with your center. Watch how he handles your "no." Watch who he becomes when your light dims or your joy goes quiet. Notice whether your boundaries make him flinch or make him respect you more.

Because no matter how perfect it looks, no love can save you from the sacred work of protecting yourself. That's your job now, and you've earned the right to do it with clarity, not apology.

You don't have to fear walking alone anymore.

Not because it's easy, but because it's honest.

And from here on out, that's the only kind of peace you'll accept — the kind you don't have to pay for with your voice, your softness, or your self-worth.

You've come home.

And you are never going back out to the cold again.

"You didn't burn it all down.

You stopped being ablaze to keep it warm."

A Tiny Favor That Helps Someone You'll Never Meet

You just finished the hard part—seeing yourself clearly and choosing peace over chaos.

Now you can help the next reader find that same relief a little faster.

Would you spend one minute helping a stranger finally exhale?

Here's what your review does, for real:

- One more woman realizes she's not crazy—just tired of carrying it all.

- One more heart learns that leaving isn't failure, it's freedom.

- One more reader feels seen instead of ashamed.

- One more person starts coming home to herself.

Your words travel further than my marketing ever could.

They tell someone scrolling at 2 a.m. that she's not alone—and that healing is possible.

What to Write (keep it simple)

- One sentence about what shifted for you.

- One line about what you're taking with you.

- Who you'd hand this book to tomorrow.

That's it. No essay. No pressure.

Just your truth.

Ready?

Point your camera at the QR code ↓

Thank you for paying it forward.

You didn't just review a book, you threw a lifeline to the next woman still holding the clipboard.

Want to Stay in Touch?

I only write when I have a new book coming out — no fluff, no spam, no performative "you got this" emails. Hand on heart!

Join the list here ↓

You'll be the first to know when the next book is out… and maybe, just maybe, it'll find you right when you need it.

References

Bancroft, L. (2002). *Why does he do that? Inside the minds of angry and controlling men.* Berkley Books.

Bowlby, J. (1988). *A secure base: Parent–child attachment and healthy human development.* Basic Books.

Brown, B. (2010). *The gifts of imperfection.* Hazelden Publishing.

Brown, B. (2021). *Atlas of the heart: Mapping meaningful connection and the language of human experience.* Random House.

Cloud, H., & Townsend, J. (1992). *Boundaries: When to say yes, how to say no to take control of your life.* Zondervan.

Crabb, C. (2021). *Men who hate therapy: Why they don't and how they can.* Penguin.

Doyle, G. (2020). *Untamed.* The Dial Press.

Fair Play: Rodsky, E. (2019). *Fair play: A game-changing solution for when you have too much to do (and more life to live).* G. P. Putnam's Sons.

Gibson, L. C. (2015). *Adult children of emotionally immature parents: How to heal from distant, rejecting, or self-involved parents.* New Harbinger Publications.

Glover, R. A. (2003). *No more Mr. Nice Guy: A proven plan for getting what you want in love, sex, and life.* Running Press.

Gottman, J., & Silver, N. (1999). *The seven principles for making marriage work.* Crown Publishers.

Hochschild, A. R., & Machung, A. (2012). *The second shift: Working families and the revolution at home* (Rev. ed.). Penguin Books.

Hooks, B. (2000). *All about love: New visions.* William Morrow.

Jay, M. (2012). *The defining decade: Why your twenties matter—and how to make the most of them now.* Twelve.

Lerner, H. (2005). *The dance of anger: A woman's guide to changing the patterns of intimate relationships.* Harper Paperbacks.

Levine, A., & Heller, R. (2010). *Attached: The new science of adult attachment and how it can help you find—and keep—love.* TarcherPerigee.

Manson, M. (2016). *The subtle art of not giving a f*ck: A counterintuitive approach to living a good life.* Harper.

Maté, G. (2003). *When the body says no: Understanding the stress-disease connection.* Vintage Canada.

Perel, E. (2006). *Mating in captivity: Unlocking erotic intelligence.* Harper.

Perel, E. (2017). *The state of affairs: Rethinking infidelity.* Harper.

Picciotto, R. (2018). *The emotionally unavailable man: A blueprint for healing.* Independently published.

Porges, S. W. (2011). *The polyvagal theory: Neurophysiological foundations of emotions, attachment, communication, and self-regulation.* W. W. Norton & Company.

Siegel, D. J. (2012). *The developing mind: How relationships and the brain interact to shape who we are* (2nd ed.). Guilford Press.

Tatkin, S. (2012). *Wired for love: How understanding your partner's brain and attachment style can help you defuse conflict and build a secure relationship.* New Harbinger Publications.

Van der Kolk, B. (2014). *The body keeps the score: Brain, mind, and body in the healing of trauma.* Viking.

www.ingramcontent.com/pod-product-compliance
Lightning Source LLC
Chambersburg PA
CBHW051440050726
47593CB00005B/1857